HAPPY LIKE
Jesus

HAPPY LIKE
Jesus

LESSONS FROM JESUS CHRIST
ON HOW TO LIVE

D. KELLY OGDEN

DESERET
BOOK

Library of Congress Cataloging-in-Publication Data
Ogden, D. Kelly (Daniel Kelly), 1947– author.
    Happy like Jesus : lessons from Jesus Christ on how to live / D. Kelly Ogden.
        p. cm.
    Includes bibliographical references and index.
    Summary: A concise look at Christlike attributes that readers can use to emulate Jesus Christ in their daily lives.
    ISBN 978-1-60908-053-2 (hardbound : alk. paper)
    1. Jesus Christ—Example. 2. Mormons—Conduct of life. I. Title.
    BT304.2.O33 2011
    232.9'04—dc22   2011001529

Printed in the United States of America
Worzalla Publishing Co., Stevens Point, WI

10   9   8   7   6   5   4   3   2   1

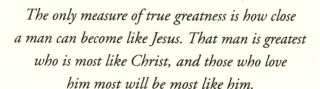

*The only measure of true greatness is how close
a man can become like Jesus. That man is greatest
who is most like Christ, and those who love
him most will be most like him.*

—President Ezra Taft Benson

Contents

Introduction

On both sides of the world the Savior taught that to have abundant life here on earth and everlasting life in heaven, we must look to him. "Seek the Lord, and ye shall live," the prophet Amos declared (Amos 5:6). Alma repeated the injunction: "Look to God and live" (Alma 37:47). And the Lord himself proclaimed, "Look unto me . . . and ye shall live" (3 Nephi 15:9).

To achieve eternal life, the kind of life our Father and our Savior live, we must learn to avoid evil. In fact, if we reverse *evil* (spell it backward), we have *live*.

In this book I consistently use the verb *to be*. In Spanish, one of the Lord's name-titles is *el Verbo* (John 1:1). He is the Verb; he is an action Verb. He says I AM, and he commands us (that's the imperative form)—YOU BE! For example, "*Ye shall be* holy; for *I am* holy" (Leviticus 11:44; emphasis added).

I also use a figure of speech called *paronomasia,* which is a play on words. The Old Testament name of Jesus, the Son of God, the second member of the Godhead, was Hebrew יהוה (YHWH, or Yehovah/Jehovah), which is a play on the Hebrew verb meaning "to be." Those four Hebrew letters (which in Greek are called the *Tetragrammaton,* meaning "Four letters") signify *I WAS, I AM,* and *I WILL BE*—all wrapped up in one word. He *is,* so he wants us also *to be.* As the heading of 3 Nephi 27 says, "Men . . . are *to be* even as Jesus *is.*"

For example, he said, "I am the light of the world" (John 8:12; 3 Nephi 9:18), and he wants us also to be the light of the world (Matthew 5:14). He walked with a lot of darkness around him, but he generated light because of personal righteousness; now he wants us to generate light because of our personal righteousness. "I am the light; I have set an example for you" (3 Nephi 18:16).

The Prophet Joseph Smith admonished us: "If you wish to go where God is, you must be like God. . . . Search your hearts, and see if you are like God. I have searched mine, and feel to repent of all my sins. . . . Is not God good? Then you be good; if he is faithful, then you be faithful."[1]

Many years ago, Dr. Charles Edward Jefferson wrote a book entitled *The Character of Jesus.* In the first pages Jefferson explains that the New Testament is more scrutinized than any other book in print. The civilization of the first century in the Holy Land has been subjected to a scrutiny and analysis that no other civilization has ever known:

"Attention is being given to the circumstances which formed the framework of [the Lord's] earthly life. Many men are working on the chronology and others are at work on the geography, and others are interested in the robe and the . . . sandals. Photographers have photographed every landscape on which he ever looked, and every scene connected with his work or career. Painters have transferred the . . . fields and lakes and skies to canvas, and . . . lecturers have made the Holy Land the most familiar spot on earth. . . . We may become so interested in the fringes and tassels of his outer life as to miss the secret which his heart has to tell. . . . It is the character of Jesus which has unique and endless significance. . . . The New Testament writers were not interested in trifles. They cared nothing for Jesus' stature, the clothes he wore, or the houses he lived in." Jefferson suggests that for more than a century scholars have been studying his circumstances when they ought to be studying him.[2]

We are now going to study him. We will take a closer look at his personality, his character traits, his teachings, and his behavior—how he acts. We will look to him and try to become like him so that we may live.

Chapter One

BE HAPPY

Despite sadness around him—and sin, pride, disbelief, hatred, and jealousy—Jesus was a happy person. Wickedness never was happiness, but righteousness always was happiness. Jesus was a righteous person and, therefore, a happy person.

President Heber C. Kimball, for many years a counselor in the First Presidency to Brigham Young, exclaimed: "I am perfectly satisfied that my Father and my God is a cheerful, pleasant, lively, and good-natured Being. Why? Because I am cheerful, pleasant, lively, and good-natured when I have His Spirit. That is one reason why I know; and another is—the Lord said, through Joseph Smith, 'I delight in a glad heart and a cheerful countenance' [D&C 59:15]. That arises from the perfection of His attributes; He is a jovial, lively person."[1]

But we might think, *How can I be a happy person with all these terrible, negative things happening around me?* Think of our

Heavenly Father and our Savior. They see much more than we do, but they maintain a joyful, positive disposition.

Jesus came to earth to teach us his way, as he said, "that your joy might be full" (John 15:11). He taught, "Ask, and ye shall receive, that your joy may be full" (John 16:24).

Jesus said, "Be of good cheer; I have overcome the world" (John 16:33). And because he has set an example for us, he is saying to us, "Now you overcome the world so you can be of good cheer."

In one of his greatest recorded sermons, Jesus describes his character in words, the Beatitudes—or "beautiful attitudes," we may call them (Matthew 5). "Blessed are ye" or "happy are ye," he taught, if you are humble in spirit, if you mourn and are compassionate, if you are meek, if you hunger and thirst after righteousness, if you are merciful and pure in heart, if you are a peacemaker, and if you are persecuted because of him. You can be happy and blessed as you develop all these characteristics of the Savior.

True disciples of Christ have an obligation to be cheerful, hopeful, and optimistic about the future. Rather than focus on the negative, God's Prophet of the Restoration counseled us:

"You have no right to take the judgments, which fell upon the ungodly before the flood, and pour them upon the head of this generation; you have no authority to use the judgments which God sent upon Pharaoh in Egypt, to terrify the inhabitants of America, neither have you any direction by commandment, to collect the calamities of six thousand years and paint them upon the curtain of these last days to scare mankind to repentance; no, you are to preach the Gospel, which is the power of God unto salvation, even glad tidings of great joy unto all people."[2]

On one occasion I spoke in a Latter-day Saint meetinghouse in Chehalis, Washington. Right across the street was a Protestant church, and in front of that church was a sign with the following message:

> We are called to be witnesses,
>
> not lawyers or judges.

As I reflected on those words, these thoughts came to mind:

1. Many other good-hearted people are with us.
2. Don't be argumentative, criticizing others; just present the truth.
3. Don't talk about Satan and his work; talk about the Savior and his work.
4. Be positive, upbeat, and optimistic.

Elder Jeffrey R. Holland has encouraged us to elevate our attitudes and reactions to what the world deals out to us: "The Lord has probably spoken enough . . . 'comforting words' to supply the whole universe, it would seem, and yet we see all around us unhappy Latter-day Saints, worried Latter-day Saints, and gloomy Latter-day Saints into whose troubled hearts not one of these innumerable consoling words seems to be allowed to enter. . . . On that very night [of Gethsemane], the night of the greatest suffering the world has ever known or ever will know, [the Savior] said, 'Peace I leave with you, my peace I give unto you. . . . Let

not your heart be troubled, neither let it be afraid' (John 14:27).
I submit to you that [this] may be one of the Savior's command-
ments that is, even in the hearts of otherwise faithful Latter-day
Saints, almost universally disobeyed."[3]

A powerful lesson comes from modern American history.
Secretary of State George C. Marshall once told a discouraged
staff, "Gentlemen, it is my experience [that] an enlisted man may
have a morale problem. [But] an officer is expected to take care of
his own morale."[4] In other words, morale problems are an enlisted
man's privilege; they are not for the officers! We are God's officers
in his kingdom. As with General Marshall's officers, so with us:
we have a duty to be positive; we have an obligation to produce
happiness, not just enjoy it.

And besides, a smile is an inexpensive way to improve your
looks! Cheerfulness is wonderfully contagious.

Remember the inspiring message of 2 Nephi 10:20:

"And now, my beloved brethren, seeing that our merciful
God has given us so great knowledge concerning these things, let
us remember him, and lay aside our sins, and *not hang down our
heads, for we are not cast off*" (emphasis added).

The *History of the Church* records an extraordinary revelation Joseph Smith received, part of which became Doctrine and
Covenants 137. In the very next paragraph after what became
section 137, the Prophet describes the following scene:

"I saw the Twelve Apostles of the Lamb, who are now upon
the earth . . . in foreign lands, standing together in a circle, much
fatigued, with their clothes tattered and feet swollen, with their

eyes cast downward, and Jesus standing in their midst, and they did not behold Him. The Savior looked upon them and wept."[5]

When you are feeling down, where are your eyes? They are looking down. Where is your head? It is hanging down. We have to keep looking up. The Savior is up there watching over us. If you will keep your head up and your eyes open, you will know that he is there to help.

President Gordon B. Hinckley was fond of saying, "Be believing. Be happy. Don't get discouraged. Things will work out."[6] How could he, and all other prophets and leaders of the Church, be so positive?

Because they have the big picture. They know what is coming. Despite all the struggles, hardships, difficulties, ordeals, even painful afflictions of this life, they know that the glorious cause of the kingdom of God will triumph. Triumph is just a little *umph* added to *try.*

We are on the winning team, so don't quit the team! Keep on keeping on. As the Savior said, "If ye know these things, happy are ye if ye do them" (John 13:17).

Stay with it, do what is right, and be happy—like Jesus.

HOLY = TO BE DEDICATED / CONSECRATED TO GOD, SACRED.

Chapter Two

BE HOLY

One day the guard in front of the Guatemala Missionary Training Center came in with a note to me as the MTC president. The note was from our next-door neighbor, a medical doctor, with his phone number and a request to call him. When I called, he said that the previous night his wife had been frightened with sounds of something striking the side of their house and their windows, and they were about to call the police. The doctor investigated and found about ten foreign coins. He realized that some of our elders were throwing coins at their house (for what reason, I can't imagine).

The next day I gathered the elders and asked who had been throwing coins at the neighbor's house. No one moved. I asked three times. Finally some hands started going up. I told them how I felt about having to go over to our neighbor and try to explain why some of our missionaries would be doing such an immature thing. They were ordained representatives of the Lord Jesus Christ and committed to behaving with quiet dignity. There is nothing dignified about tossing coins at the neighbor's house!

It turned out to be a lesson in spiritual maturity. What is our ultimate goal? To get to the celestial kingdom? No, not just to get to a place. Rather, it is to become like Heavenly Father and our Savior, and the place will take care of itself.

Our Heavenly Father and our Savior are holy, and they expect us to become holy also. We can learn something profound from the book of Leviticus, the handbook of the Levitical priests who served former-day Saints in the Mosaic dispensation:

"Ye shall be holy; for I am holy" (11:44).
"Ye shall be holy: for I the Lord your God am holy" (19:2).
"Be ye holy: for I am the Lord your God" (20:7).
"Ye shall be holy unto me: for I the Lord am holy" (20:26).

The Lord clearly has great expectations for those who are called and set apart for his work.

The next day I received a note from one of the guilty missionaries. The note itself shows why I love these humble missionaries, who are learning and growing. The elder wrote (my translation):

"When you called us elders into the general meeting room because of the foolish thing we had done the night before, and then talked with us like a father, I felt pretty bad because I had disappointed not only my Heavenly Father but also you. Because of the sadness I felt last night when I went to bed, I cried half the night until I finally felt at peace. President, I love you and Hermana [Sister] Ogden as my father and mother. The feelings I have for you come from my heart, not just my lips. I wrote to my mother also about the foolish thing I had done, and as I wrote, tears fell on my letter to her." Then he bore his testimony of Jesus Christ and how he loves and forgives.[1]

Our Redeemer has taught us how to be holy, and he has shown us the way.[2] By immersing ourselves in his words and sincerely talking each day with our Heavenly Father, along with giving selfless service to our brothers and sisters and offering faithful service to God in his House, we can be holy—like Jesus.

Chapter Three

BE SPIRITUALLY MINDED

After the Savior was baptized, Matthew records that "Jesus was led up of the Spirit, into the wilderness, to be with God" (JST, Matthew 4:1). Later, temptations came, but he gave no heed to them (D&C 20:22). He was so full of the Spirit that the devil had no effect on him.

He had gone into the wilderness to commune with the Infinite, to set aside the things of the flesh, and to prepare for his ministry through empowerment of the Holy Ghost. All of us may, as we travel through this wilderness of mortal life, follow his example and do the same: fill ourselves daily (especially through scripture study and prayer) so that when temptations come—as they inevitably will—they will have no power to overcome us because we are, like our Exemplar, filled with the Spirit.

Matthew tells us that when the devil who tempted Jesus left him, "angels came and ministered unto him" (Matthew 4:11). The same can happen to us as we follow his way. By filling ourselves with the Spirit through his words (scriptures) and our words (prayers), we displace the powers of worldliness with the powers of heaven. The devil will leave us, and angels will come. Yes, *heavenly* angels can come, but *mortal* angels will come—the Lord will send someone into our life to give us a lift just when we need it.

There is a pattern to follow in Jesus' life and ministry. Like him, we must forsake the world, be born again of water and of the Spirit, and thus enter the kingdom of God (John 3:3, 5).

President Boyd K. Packer tells the dramatic story of his mother following the whisperings of the Spirit:

"Many years ago my parents lived on a little farm. It was a poor farm. One day my father was plowing and he broke the plow. He came to the house to tell mother he had to take the plow to town to be welded. Mother was washing, with water on the stove. She hurried and got the children ready. She didn't go to town very often, and was anxious to go. Father hitched the horse to the buggy and brought it to the door. She lifted the children into the buggy.

"As she went to climb in, she hesitated. 'I don't think I will go with you today,' she said to my father.

"'What's the matter?' Father asked.

"'I don't know,' she answered. 'I just have the feeling that I shouldn't go.'

"When she said the word *feeling* that meant something to my father. He was wise enough not to talk her out of it.

"'Well, if you have that feeling, perhaps you had better stay home.'

"She lifted the children out of the buggy, and of course, you know what they started to do. She stood and watched as the buggy went down the road, the children crying with disappointment. And then she said to herself, 'Now wasn't that silly of me.' She returned to the house to finish the washing.

"She had only been in the house a few minutes when she smelled smoke. The house was afire up in the ceiling. The children formed a bucket brigade and soon they had the fire out. And so ends an ordinary incident; except when you ask a question, Why didn't she go to town that day?

"My mother prayed earnestly that the Lord would bless them that they could feed and clothe their children. They were saving money to pay for the farm. The money was in the house. If the house had burned, they would have lost everything. . . .

"She stayed home because of a feeling. A still, small voice had spoken to her. . . . And this is my counsel to you. . . . <u>Learn to live by the Spirit.</u>"[1]

Living by the Spirit, we plant good seeds that can grow, mature, and become fruitful. But good seeds can perish if they don't sink some deep roots and avoid being choked by thorns. We can start out well, but we have to *continue* in the Lord's ways, consciously working to expel the worldliness that incessantly encroaches in our life. The spiritually minded receive the seed, which is the word of God.

"They [who fall on rock] hear, receive the word with joy; [but] have no root, which for a while believe, and in time of temptation fall away.

"And that which fell among thorns are they, which, when

they have heard, go forth, and are choked with cares and riches and pleasures of this life, and bring no fruit to perfection" (Luke 8:13–14).

As the Lord taught us through the Prophet Joseph Smith, some people get their hearts set so much on the things of this world—becoming choked with the cares, riches, and pleasures of this life—that they separate themselves from the "powers of heaven," they abandon the "principles of righteousness," and they "undertake to cover [their] sins." As a result, the "heavens withdraw themselves" (D&C 121:35–37).

Getting things seems to be a major temptation for humans. How foolish it is to spend so much time and effort getting things, only to leave them all behind when we die and return to our God. "Beware of covetousness," Jesus warned, "for a man's life consisteth not in the abundance of the things which he possesseth. . . . So is he that layeth up treasure for himself, and is not rich toward God" (Luke 12:15, 21). The psalmist tersely describes why this is so foolish: "When he dieth he shall carry nothing away: [his riches] shall not descend after him" (Psalm 49:17). Think about the implications of the word *descend* in that verse!

Now we continue to examine the pattern of Jesus' life and ministry: he entered into the kingdom (baptism), he filled himself daily with the Spirit (scriptures and prayer), and then, as John tells us, "Jesus went up into the temple and taught" (John 7:14). "And early in the morning he came again into the temple, and all the people came unto him; and he sat down, and taught them" (John 8:2). In our case we go to the temple, sit down, and are taught (by the same Lord Jesus). One of the best ways to maintain our proper direction is through regular worship in the temple: making sacred covenants, participating in essential ordinances, and receiving further instructions. The temple helps us keep our priorities straight.

President Packer spoke to the men and women of the Church Educational System on February 6, 2004, from the Salt Lake Tabernacle. He said some things to forty thousand religious educators that he repeated a few days later, verbatim, to thousands of Latter-day Saint lawyers and judges all over the world:

"The world is spiraling downward at an ever-quickening pace. I am sorry to tell you that it will not get better.

"It is my purpose to *charge* each of you . . . with the responsibility—to put you on alert. These are days of great spiritual danger. . . .

"I know of nothing in the history of the Church or in the history of the world to compare with our present circumstances. [Nothing happened in Sodom and Gomorrah which exceeds in wickedness and depravity that which surrounds us now.]

"Words of profanity, vulgarity, and blasphemy are heard everywhere. Unspeakable wickedness and perversion were once hidden in dark places; now they are in the open, even accorded legal protection.

"At Sodom and Gomorrah these things were localized. Now they are spread across the world, and they are among us. . . .

"Satan uses every intrigue to disrupt the family. The sacred relationship between man and woman, husband and wife, through which mortal bodies are conceived and life is passed to the next generation, is being showered with filth. Surely you can see what the adversary is about. The first line of defense, the home, is crumbling."[2]

But President Packer also reminded us how we can avoid all this worldliness and persevere in being spiritually minded: "Our labors in the temple cover us with a shield and a protection, both individually and as a people."[3]

David Galbraith has been my closest friend for many years. His father was not active in the Church during David's growing-up years. One day his father was in the pool hall (the usual place to find him) with a cup of coffee on the corner pocket of a pool table and a cigarette in hand. His priesthood leader, J. Golden Snow, came in and asked to talk with him and then called him into the bishopric! David, at age twelve, was already stealing cigarettes and going out behind the barn to smoke. But because someone had a little inspired foresight, lives were changed. His father was called on the spot to abandon his worldly ways and become more spiritually minded. He gave up his vices and served faithfully as a counselor and then as a bishop for the next seventeen years, and his sons and daughters have gone on to serve in extraordinary ways throughout the world.

The moral of this story is, Somebody can make a difference.

And the message for all of us is, Avoid worldliness and be spiritually minded—like Jesus.

Chapter Four

BE HUMBLE

All power was given to the Savior in heaven and earth (Matthew 28:18). He took all that power and submitted himself. "Learn of me; for I am meek and lowly in heart," Jesus said (Matthew 11:29). He wants us to become as he is; therefore we too must become meek and lowly in heart. Again, he wants us to look to him and live. We can either look and live, or we can be proud and perish.

A splendid example of the humble disciple is the forerunner, the great prophet who prepared the way for the Anointed One, the friend of the Bridegroom. John the Baptist humbly declared, "He must increase, but I must decrease" (John 3:30).

Now there is a remarkable illustration of one who had learned to control his ego and his pride. John was recognized as the first real prophet—in the land of prophets—to appear on the scene in centuries. For months he taught hundreds, maybe thousands, from all parts of the land of Israel and neighboring lands, stirring up some notoriety with the Jewish leadership in Jerusalem. In fact, he had been training future Apostles, including John and Andrew and probably others of the Twelve, as well as others who would carry his message of repentance and baptism throughout the Mediterranean world (John 1:35–42; Acts 1:21–22).[1]

But the day Jesus arrived at the River Jordan, John put himself in his proper place and immediately transferred loyalty to the Savior, the Son of God, saying, "He that cometh from heaven is above all" (John 3:31). Jesus taught us to live not for the glory of men, or to "be seen of men" (Matthew 6:5; see also 23:5), but to pay our devotions to God quietly and without fanfare, doing kind things anonymously without seeking recognition (Matthew 6:5; see also 23:5). Our priority, he said, is to seek first to build the kingdom of God, not our own little kingdom.

I learned a wonderful lesson in three words from Elder David B. Haight of the Quorum of the Twelve Apostles. I taught many missionaries to post by the door of their room a sign on which those three words were written: "I AM THIRD." The missionaries always looked a little puzzled and curious, so I explained that God must be first in our life and labors, our fellow humans should be second, and we need to be *third*. We get into trouble when we put ourselves in first place. It is best to put our hand in the hand of God and let him work with us according to his plan.

Our modern apostles and prophets are wonderfully adept at teaching us about the Savior's way of doing things. President Henry B. Eyring warned: "Make sure you don't focus too much on yourself or your personal problems and struggles. Instead of thinking of yourself primarily as someone who is seeking purification, think of yourself as someone who is trying to find out who around you needs your help."[2] Elder David A. Bednar cautioned: "We must be careful to remember in our service that we are conduits and channels; we are not the light. 'For it is not ye that speak, but the Spirit of your Father which speaketh in you' (Matthew 10:20). It is never about me and it is never about you. In fact, anything you or I do as an instructor that knowingly and intentionally draws attention to self . . . is a form of priestcraft that inhibits the teaching effectiveness of the Holy Ghost."[3]

President Hugh B. Brown, then of the Quorum of the Twelve Apostles, told a story about himself that has become a classic in Latter-day Saint literature. Entitled "The Currant Bush," it is an extraordinary example of how we must humble ourselves and submit to the will of God:

"You sometimes wonder if you know better than [the Lord] does about what you ought to do and ought to become. I am wondering if I may tell you a story . . . that is older than you are. It's a piece out of my own life. . . . It has to do with an incident in my life when God showed me that *he knew best.*

"I was living up in Canada. I had purchased a farm. It was run-down. I went out one morning and saw a currant bush. It had grown up over six feet high. It was going all to wood. There were no blossoms and no currants. I was raised on a fruit farm in Salt Lake before we went to Canada, and I knew what ought to happen to that currant bush. So I got some pruning shears and went after it, and I cut it down, and pruned it, and clipped it back until there was nothing left but a little clump of stumps. It was just coming daylight, and I thought I saw on top of each of these little stumps what appeared to be a tear, and I thought the currant bush was crying. I was kind of simpleminded (and I haven't entirely gotten over it), and I looked at it, and smiled, and said, 'What are you crying about?' You know, I thought I heard that currant bush talk. And I thought I heard it say this: 'How could you do this to me? I was making such wonderful growth. I was almost as big as the shade tree and the fruit tree that are inside the fence, and now you have cut me down. Every plant in the garden will look down on me, because I didn't make what I should have made. How *could* you do this to me? I thought you were the gardener here.' That's what I thought I heard the currant bush say, and I thought it so much that I answered. I said, 'Look, little currant bush, I *am* the gardener here, and I know what I want you to be. I didn't intend you to be a fruit tree or a shade tree. I want you to be a currant bush, and some day, little currant bush, when you are laden with fruit, you are going to say, "Thank you, Mr. Gardener, for loving me enough to cut me down, for caring enough about me to hurt me. Thank you, Mr. Gardener."'

"Years passed, and I found myself in England. I was in command of a cavalry unit in the Canadian Army. I had made rather rapid progress as far as promotions are concerned, and I held the rank of field officer in the British Canadian Army. And I was proud of my position. And there was an opportunity for me to become a general. I had taken all the examinations. I had the seniority. There was just one man between me and that which for ten years I had hoped to get, the office of general in the British Army. I swelled up with pride. And this one man became a casualty, and I received a telegram from London. It said: 'Be in my office tomorrow morning at 10:00,' signed by General Turner in charge of all Canadian forces. I called in my valet, my personal servant. I told him to polish my buttons, to brush my hat and my boots, and to make me look like a general because that is what I was going to be. He did the best he could with what he had to work on, and I went up to London. I walked smartly into the office of the General, and I saluted him smartly, and he gave me the same kind of a salute a senior officer usually gives—a sort of 'Get out of the way, worm!' He said, 'Sit down, Brown.' Then he said, 'I'm sorry I cannot make the appointment. You are entitled to it. You have passed all the examinations. You have the seniority. You've been a good officer, but I can't make the appointment. You are to return to Canada and become a training officer and a transport officer. Someone else will be made a general.' That for which I had been hoping and praying for ten years suddenly slipped out of my fingers.

"Then he went into the other room to answer the telephone, and I took a soldier's privilege of looking on his desk. I saw my personal history sheet. Right across the bottom of it in bold, block-type letters was written, 'THIS MAN IS A MORMON.' We were not very well liked in those days. When I saw that, I knew why I had not been appointed. I already held the highest rank of any Mormon in the British Army. He came back and said, 'That's all, Brown.' I saluted him again, but not quite as smartly. I saluted out of duty and went out. I got on the train and started back to my town, 120 miles away, with a broken heart, with bitterness in my soul. And every click of the wheels on the rails seemed to say, 'You are a failure. You will be called a coward when you get home. You raised all those Mormon boys to join the army, then you sneak off home.' I knew what I was going to get, and when I got to my tent, I was so bitter that I threw my cap and my saddle brown belt on the cot. I clinched my fists and I shook them at heaven. I said, 'How could you do this to me, God? I have done everything I could do to measure up. There is nothing that I could have done—that I should have done—that I haven't done. How could you do this to me?' I was as bitter as gall.

"And then I heard a voice, and I recognized the tone of this voice. It was my own voice, and the voice said, 'I am the gardener here. I know what I want you to do.' The bitterness went out of my soul, and I fell on my knees by the cot to ask forgiveness for my ungratefulness and my bitterness. While kneeling there I heard a song being sung in an adjoining tent. A number of Mormon boys met regularly every Tuesday night. I usually met with them. We would sit on the floor and have a Mutual Improvement Association. As I was kneeling there, praying for forgiveness, I heard their voices singing:

> *It may not be on the mountain height*
> *Or over the stormy sea;*
> *It may not be at the battle's front*
> *My Lord will have need of me;*
> *But if, by a still, small voice he calls*
> *To paths that I do not know,*
> *I'll answer, dear Lord, with my hand in thine:*
> *I'll go where you want me to go.* [Hymns, no. 270]

"I arose from my knees a humble man. And now, almost fifty years later, I look up to him and say, 'Thank you, Mr. Gardener, for cutting me down, for loving me enough to hurt me.' I see now that it was wise that I should not become a general at that time, because if I had I would have been senior officer of all western Canada, with a lifelong, handsome salary, a place to live, and a pension when I'm no good any longer, but I would have raised my six daughters and two sons in army barracks. They would no doubt have married out of the Church, and I think I would not have amounted to anything. I haven't amounted to very much as it is, but I have done better than I would have done if the Lord had let me go the way I wanted to go.

"I wanted to tell you that oft-repeated story because there are many of you who are going to have some very difficult experiences: disappointment, heartbreak, bereavement, defeat. You are going to be tested and tried to prove what you are made of. I just want you to know that if you don't get what you think you ought to get, remember, 'God is the gardener here. He knows what he wants you to be.' Submit yourselves to his will."[4]

So, as the scriptures teach and as Elder Brown's story illustrates, be submissive, be meek and lowly, and be humble—like Jesus.

Chapter Five

BE
KNOWLEDGEABLE

Knowledge is power. Certainly the witness of the Spirit is the surest foundation, but there is nothing wrong with a knowledge-solid testimony. Please pardon the expression, but in the Church we need more than "punch and cookie" testimonies. Spirituality is not born of ignorance. The more knowledge we have, the stronger our spiritual witness can be. Someone has suggested that the Latter-day Saints know the gospel is true, but they don't know the gospel. We should know the reasons that we believe what we believe.

Knowledge of any truth is valuable, whatever the nature and whatever the source. Joseph Smith had an indefatigable appetite for learning in all disciplines. When he organized the school of the prophets in Kirtland, Ohio, in the mid-1830s, students there studied everything from history, politics, geography, and religious texts to cultures, languages (German, Greek, Hebrew, whatever they could get their hands on), and even English grammar. They just couldn't get enough of learning of every kind. We would do well to follow their example.

Another of my favorite stories is an episode from the life of Dr. Louis Agassiz, whose proxy temple ordinances were performed in the St. George Utah Temple in 1877, which means he can now be counted among the Saints of God.[1] I take the following account from Elder Marion D. Hanks, who served as an Assistant to the Quorum of the Twelve Apostles and later as a member of the Seventy.

"[It is] the story of an obscure spinster woman who insisted that she never had a chance. She muttered these words to Dr. Louis Agassiz, distinguished naturalist, after one of his lectures in London. In response to her complaint, he replied: 'Do you say, madam, you never had a chance? What do you do?'

"'I am single and help my sister run a boardinghouse.'

"'What do you do?' he asked.

"'I skin potatoes and chop onions.'

"He said, 'Madam, where do you sit during these interesting but homely duties?'

"'On the bottom step of the kitchen stairs.'

"'Where do your feet rest?'

"'On the glazed brick.'

"'What is glazed brick?'

"'I don't know, sir.'

"He said, 'How long have you been sitting there?'

"She said, 'Fifteen years.'

"'Madam, here is my personal card,' said Dr. Agassiz. 'Would you kindly write me a letter concerning the nature of a glazed brick?'

"She took him seriously. She went home and explored the dictionary and discovered that a brick was a piece of baked clay. That definition seemed too simple to send to Dr. Agassiz, so after the dishes were washed, she went to the library and in an encyclopedia read that a glazed brick is vitrified kaolin and hydrous aluminum silicate. She didn't know what that meant, but she was curious and found out. She took the word *vitrified* and read all she could find about it. Then she visited museums. She moved out of the basement of her life and into a new world on the wings of *vitrified*. And having started, she took the word *hydrous*, studied geology, and went back in her studies to the time when God started the world and laid the clay beds. One afternoon she went to a brickyard, where she found the history of more than 120 kinds of bricks and tiles, and why there have to be so many. Then she sat down and wrote thirty-six pages on the subject of glazed brick and tile.

"Back came the letter from Dr. Agassiz: 'Dear Madam, this is the best article I have ever seen on the subject. If you will kindly change the three words marked with asterisks, I will have it published and pay you for it.'

"A short time later there came a letter that brought $250, and penciled on the bottom of this letter was this query: 'What was under those bricks?' She had learned the value of time and answered with a single word: 'Ants.' He wrote back and said, 'Tell me about the ants.'

"She began to study ants. She found there were between

eighteen hundred and twenty-five hundred different kinds. There are ants so tiny you could put three head-to-head on a pin and have standing room left over for other ants; ants an inch long that march in solid armies half a mile wide, driving everything ahead of them; ants that are blind; ants that get wings on the afternoon of the day they die; ants that build anthills so tiny that you can cover one with a lady's silver thimble; peasant ants that keep cows to milk, and then deliver the fresh milk to the apartment house of the aristocrat ants of the neighborhood.

"After wide reading, much microscopic work, and deep study, the spinster sat down and wrote Dr. Agassiz 360 pages on the subject. He published the book and sent her the money, and she went to visit all the lands of her dreams on the proceeds of her work."

The article concludes with a quotation from Lord Chesterton: "'There are no uninteresting things; there are only uninterested people.'"[2]

Our Savior wants us to begin right here on earth our eternal quest for knowledge, especially knowledge of God and godly things.

Martin Masariego from El Salvador did just that. A short, powerfully humble man, he told the missionaries at the Guatemala MTC that he first learned about the Church in 1978.

"He was twenty-six years old and wore long hair, bracelets, and a necklace. He was a member of another Christian faith but had been unhappy with the answers he received as to where mankind had come from, why we were here on earth, and where we would be going. When he was younger he had asked these questions of his priest, who had responded that he would understand when he was older. As a young man Martin began attending other churches and the local Jewish synagogue. He studied with the agnostics. No one could give satisfactory answers to his questions, not even his mother, who also told him to just be patient.

"One day two Latter-day Saint missionaries from North America knocked on his door. He opened it; they introduced themselves and then said, 'We are here to answer your questions.' He asked, 'What are my questions?' They replied, 'You want to know where you came from, why you are here, and where you are going after this life.' Martin was immediately interested and invited them in.

"He loved what they shared, especially about the priesthood. His wife didn't want to listen, but the missionaries wouldn't teach him without her. They asked him to ask his wife if they could leave a blessing on the home. She agreed. The missionaries used the authority of God to call down a blessing on the couple and their children. The prayer must have softened her heart because at the end the missionaries asked her when they could return to give the first lesson. She invited them back. Martin called that a miracle, especially since he and his wife were on the verge of a separation.

"The Masariegos soon joined the Church and served faithfully. Brother Masariego was later called to serve in the temple presidency in Guatemala."[3]

The Lord has sent knowledge to the earth, even of the weighty questions of eternity, the most precious of all knowledge. He wants us to have all the additional light and knowledge we can accept and live.

Following strongly worded exchanges with his antagonists, Jesus asked them, "What think ye of Christ? *whose son* is he?" (Matthew 22:42; emphasis added). It is imperative to have a correct answer to that vital question. Jesus taught through the words of his Intercessory Prayer that "life eternal" is to "know thee the only true God [the Father], and Jesus Christ," whom he has sent (John 17:3). Jesus had already taught Nicodemus that whoso believed in the Son of God would "not perish, but have everlasting life" (John 3:16). He taught his followers to "believe that Jesus is the Christ, the Son of God; and that believing ye might have life through his name" (John 20:31). That is the ultimate knowledge, the most essential of all.

That greatest knowledge comes through studying his words: "Search the scriptures; for . . . they are they which testify of me" (John 5:39; see also verses 45–47). "The words that I speak unto you, they are spirit, and they are life" (John 6:63).

Right after Jesus taught the strong doctrine that he is the Bread of Life and that unless we are willing to partake of him, we have no life in us (John 6:53), John recorded that "many of his disciples went back, and walked no more with him. Then said Jesus unto the twelve, Will ye also go away? Then Simon Peter answered him, Lord, to whom shall we go? thou hast the words of eternal life. And we believe and are sure that thou art that Christ, the Son of the living God" (John 6:66–69).

The scriptures, containing the words of God through his prophets, and the temples, where we are endowed with knowledge directly from the Father and the Son, are two of our best sources of the knowledge of God.

How do the words of Christ come to us when we need them? "The Comforter, which is the Holy Ghost, whom the Father will send in my name, he shall teach you all things and bring all things to your remembrance, whatsoever I have said unto you" (John 14:26).

The Holy Spirit, symbolized by fire, burns the knowledge of God deep into our souls. The two disciples walking the road to Emmaus had that very experience. They exclaimed, "Did not our heart burn within us, while he talked with us . . . and while he opened to us the scriptures?" (Luke 24:32).

This revelation of the knowledge of God, which can and must come to every soul seeking exaltation, is a sure foundation; it is the rock of our salvation. Jesus said, "Upon this rock I will build my church; and the gates of hell shall not prevail against it" (Matthew 16:18).

Have you ever thought about the gates of hell? It is curious how many times the Lord refers to them. In 3 Nephi 18:13 he warns that "the gates of hell are ready open to receive [us]." These days some of the gates of hell are pornography, aberrant sexual relationships, selfishness, greed, pride, and other forms of severe worldliness. These gates of hell are gaping wide to swallow anyone who lacks the Spirit and who gets close enough to be drawn in.

Knowing God and his truths is absolutely urgent in order to escape the bombardment of worldliness surrounding us. The knowledge of God, including his ordinances and covenants, becomes our shield and protection against the powers of darkness.

So in all your getting, get knowledge. Come to know God, and become knowledgeable—like Jesus.

Chapter Six

BE SERVICEABLE

We have all been called to serve. True greatness can be measured by your service ability. Jesus explained, "Ye know that the princes of the Gentiles exercise dominion over them, and they that are great exercise authority upon them. But it shall not be so among you: but whosoever will be great among you, let him be your minister; and whosoever will be chief among you, let him be your servant: even as the Son of man came not to be ministered unto, but to minister, and to give his life" (Matthew 20:25–28; see also Luke 22:24–27).

Jesus expects us to give our life also: "Greater love hath no man than this, that a man lay down his life for his friends" (John 15:13). Laying down our life doesn't just mean dying for others; it also means living for them, being willing to sacrifice (give up) our time and effort to bless others. "He that is greatest among you shall be your servant" (Matthew 23:11).

We often think that the greatest among us are those who are

presidents, directors, chief executives, and others who hold titles of leadership. Jesus, on the other hand, said, "I am among you as he that serveth" (Luke 22:27). If those who are leaders are truly *serving* as leaders, they *are* great—according to the Lord's definition of greatness.

"Then said Jesus unto his disciples, If any man will come after me, let him deny himself, and take up his cross, and follow me. For whosoever will save his life shall lose it: and whosoever will lose his life for my sake shall find it" (Matthew 16:24–25; see also Luke 9:23–24).

Losing ourselves in the service of others is serving God. Someone penned this provocative refrain:

> *I sought my God, but my God I could not see;*
> *I sought my soul, but my soul eluded me;*
> *I sought my brother, and I found all three.*

Losing ourselves in the service of God and his children results in great blessings. "If any man serve me, him will my Father honour" (John 12:26).

Here are some examples of men who gave their lives in service to Jesus during his lifetime: James and John, sons of Zebedee, "forsook all, and followed him" (Luke 5:11). Matthew Levi "left all, rose up, and followed him" (Luke 5:28).

"A certain ruler asked him [Jesus], saying, Good Master, what shall I do to inherit eternal life?" Jesus reviewed with him the basic commandments that had been around for centuries. "And he [the ruler] said, All these have I kept from my youth up. Now when Jesus heard these things, he said unto him, Yet lackest thou one thing: sell all that thou hast, and distribute unto the poor, and thou shalt have treasure in heaven: and come, follow me" (Luke 18:18, 21–22).

Treasures in heaven are far grander than any accumulated treasures on earth. This rich ruler may have had such potential. Who knows? Maybe he could even have become one of the leaders of Christ's Church. But he apparently declined Jesus' invitation to sacrifice and serve. On the other hand, Peter announced, "Lo, we have left all, and followed thee. And [Jesus] said unto them, . . . There is no man that hath left house, or parents, or brethren, or wife, or children, for the kingdom of God's sake, who shall not receive manifold more in this present time, and in the world to come life everlasting" (Luke 18:28–30).

There is no way to get the God of heaven in our debt. He is the prolific paymaster, the abundant rewarder of whoever does good. Latter-day Saint gospel scholar Andrew Skinner described God's offer in this way: "The magnitude of the promise is incomprehensible and the unevenness of the offer staggering: everything we possess in exchange for everything God possesses."[1]

But here is a word of caution. It is possible to lose ourselves in the service of others *for the wrong motive,* such as just to secure earthly and heavenly rewards.

A man called me at my office at Brigham Young University three times in two days concerned about *chosenness*—about having one's calling and election made sure. He said he had been studying these matters for years and was confused and worried.

After talking with him for some time, I sensed that he was

excessively preoccupied with this one doctrine and shared with him something I recalled reading in *The Words of Joseph Smith.* It was an entry from Willard Richards, who copied into what he called his Pocket Companion the notes others had made of Joseph Smith's sermons. In an address sometime before August 8, 1839, referring to John 14:23, the Prophet commented on the elevated concepts of the Father and the Son abiding with a righteous person, and about perfection, the Holy Spirit of Promise, and being sealed up to eternal life. An endnote says:

"As Joseph Smith here defines it, making one's calling and election sure is the crowning achievement of a life of righteous devotion. However, the Prophet apparently senses that if this concept is too commonly taught it could easily generate within the Church a misguided devotion to a principle that could divert the Saints' energy from the equally important principle of selfless devotion to others. Seeking blessings for oneself only is contrary to the principle that 'He that loseth his life for my sake shall find it' (Matthew 10:39)."[2]

At one of the most sacred occasions of his mortal ministry, Jesus spoke these poignant words to his best friends, to whom he was about to leave the leadership of his kingdom:

"Ye call me Master and Lord: and ye say well; for so I am. If I then, your Lord and Master, have washed your feet; ye also ought to wash one another's feet. For I have given you an example, that ye should do as I have done to you. Verily, verily, I say unto you, The servant is not greater than his lord; neither he that is sent greater than he that sent him" (John 13:13–16).

The words "he that is sent" is Greek *apostolos.* The Apostle certainly was not greater than the Master. If the Good Shepherd came "as he that serveth" (Luke 22:27), then every good undershepherd must do no less.

We are to give of ourselves unselfishly, constantly finding opportunities to lift and help to bear the burdens of others. Becoming a perennial giver brings happiness to the server and the served.

One day our daughter Elizabeth blogged this simple, down-to-earth lesson to us:

"I have Swiss chard growing in my garden. Four beautiful, green heads of Swiss chard. I didn't even know what Swiss chard was until my mother-in-law planted it in my garden. I love it. It is just my kind of plant. One day I went out and harvested a huge armful of leaves and stuffed them into a pan to steam with curry powder, ground cumin, and butter. Delicious! But the best thing about this vegetable, and the thing that makes it most compatible with me, is that it is self-replenishing. I take and take and it just keeps right on growing. None of this nurturing and watering and caring for a single head of lettuce only to have to pluck it out and wait for another seed to grow in its place. I appreciate my Swiss chard because it is low-maintenance, a giver, and self-sufficient. So thanks, Mary, for introducing me to my perfect plant-mate. We'll have a happy life I'm sure."

You have been called to serve, which means you give and give and give. In fact, you are not happy if you are not serving others. Your assignment is to change lives, and because your exposure to each passing person in life is often brief, it is wise to touch them quickly and deeply. During your early years on earth, you had parents, teachers, leaders, and older friends and relatives whose duty was to create a spiritual atmosphere for you to flourish in; now it is your turn to serve by creating a spiritual atmosphere for others. That is what we call leadership. You are called to be a leader and to be continuously serviceable—like Jesus.

Chapter Seven

BE PRAYERFUL

The Savior wants us to be full; for instance, he wants us to be prayerful and peaceful and fruitful. These characteristics will be the topics of the next three chapters.

Jesus sometimes began his day by rising early and finding a solitary place to pray. "And in the morning, rising up a great while before day, he went out, and departed into a solitary place, and there prayed" (Mark 1:35). During his three-year mission, he repeatedly and deliberately set aside hours of solitude during which he prayed to Heavenly Father and rejuvenated his spirit:

"And when it was day, he departed and went into a desert place" (Luke 4:42). "And he withdrew himself into the wilderness, and prayed" (Luke 5:16). "He went out into a mountain to pray, and continued all night in prayer to God" (Luke 6:12). Other examples are found in Matthew 14:23; 17:1; 26:36; Luke 9:18; and John 6:15.

Although Jesus was incessantly pressed upon by multitudes

and many times forced to go without food and sleep, in key moments he would find solitude and commune with his Father in preparation for more spiritual labor. He also prepared the future leaders of his Church: "He took Peter and John and James, and went up into a mountain to pray" (Luke 9:28). Even during the agony of Gethsemane, Jesus admonished his Apostles, "Rise and pray, lest ye enter into temptation" (Luke 22:46). Actually, that is one of the grand purposes of prayer: we cannot succumb to temptation while we are engaged in sincere communication with our Father, so prayer is key to avoid ruining ourselves with sin.

On a certain day the disciples asked Jesus how to pray. He not only gave them a model prayer but also taught them through a parable to seek God—as the friend at midnight—with "importunity" (Luke 11:8). The verb *importune* means "to request with urgency; to press with solicitation; to urge with frequent or unceasing application."[1]

Jesus' story relates how a guest dropped in on a man in the middle of the night, and the man, realizing he had no food to offer his guest at that hour, attempted to wake up his sleeping neighbor to borrow three loaves of bread. Though a friend, the neighbor was reluctant to arise at that hour but finally—because of the persistence of the would-be borrower—got up to answer the need.

The point of the parable is the importance of importuning—persisting in imploring for what we want from God. The parable is followed by the frequent injunction: "Knock, and it shall be opened unto you. . . . And to him that knocketh it shall be opened" (Luke 11:9–10). God wants us to pray, plead, implore, and *importune*—specifically, frequently, and sincerely. He wants us to plead with him in humility for what we need. In the Joseph Smith Translation, the parable of the friend at midnight begins with a simple but powerful promise: *"Your heavenly Father will not fail to give unto you whatsoever ye ask of him"* (JST, Luke 11:5; emphasis added). The message is, "Don't give up or despair; keep asking." In this case the repetition is not vain repetition. As the Prophet Joseph Smith said, "Come to God [and] weary him until he blesses you."[2]

Jesus taught more about this important principle of being prayerful with another parable, this time about an unjust judge (Luke 18:1–8). The issue that drew this parable from the Lord is stated in verse 1: "Men ought always to pray, and not to faint" (not to faint means not to give up, not to despair). The story is sometimes called the parable of the importunate widow. The parable teaches the same lesson as the parable of the friend at midnight: perseverance and persistence in prayer. Keep on importuning the throne of God, and he will eventually answer. Sometimes God insists that we keep importuning because he knows we are not ready for the requested answer or blessing—at least, *not yet.* We keep asking not until he is ready but until *we* are ready.

God is telling you to keep pleading. "Thy prayers . . . have come up into my ears," and they will be answered "according to thy petition" (D&C 90:1). You must keep asking.

President Hugh B. Brown, then a member of the First Presidency, recounted an experience with mighty prayer earlier in his life:

"In 1904 I went to England on a mission. . . . When I got into Norwich the president of the district sent me down to Cambridge. He said, '. . . There is not another Latter-day Saint within 120 miles of Cambridge, so you will be alone.' He said, 'You might be interested to know, Brother Brown, that the last Mormon elder that was in Cambridge was driven out by a mob at the point of a gun and was told the next Mormon elder that stepped inside the city limits would be shot on sight.' He said, 'I thought you would be glad to know that.' . . .

"[I] went to Cambridge. . . . I went out on Friday morning and tracted all morning without any response except a slammed door in my face. I tracted all afternoon with the same response, and I came home pretty well discouraged. But I decided to tract Saturday morning. . . . I went out and tracted all morning and got the same results. I came home dejected and downhearted, and I thought I ought to go home. I thought the Lord had made a mistake in sending me to Cambridge. . . .

"I was feeling sorry for myself, and I heard a knock at the front door. The lady of the house answered the door. I heard a voice say, 'Is there an Elder Brown lives here?' . . .

"He came in and said, 'Are you Elder Brown?'

"I was not surprised that he was surprised. I said, 'Yes, sir.'

"He said, 'Did you leave this tract at my door?' . . .

"I said, 'Yes, sir, I did.'

"He said, 'Last Sunday there were seventeen of us heads of families left the Church of England. . . . We decided that we would pray all through the week that the Lord would send us a new pastor. When I came home tonight I was discouraged; I thought our prayer had not been answered. But when I found this tract under my door, I knew the Lord had answered our prayer. Will you come tomorrow night and be our new pastor?'

"Now, I hadn't been in the mission field three days. I didn't know anything about missionary work, and he wanted me to be their pastor. . . .

"He left. . . . I went up to my room and prepared for bed. I knelt at my bed. My young brothers and sisters, for the first time in my life I talked with God. I told Him of my predicament. I pleaded for his help. . . . I got up and went to bed and couldn't sleep and got out and prayed again, and kept that up all night—but I really talked with God.

"The next morning . . . I went up on the campus in Cambridge and walked all morning. . . . Then I walked all afternoon. . . . I came back to my room at 6:00 and I sat there meditating, worrying, wondering. . . . Finally it came to the point where the clock said 6:45. I got up and . . . dragged myself down to that building, literally. . . .

"Just as I got to the gate the man came out, the man I had seen the night before. He bowed very politely and said, 'Come in, Reverend, sir.' I had never been called that before. I went in and saw the room filled with people, and they all stood up to honor their new pastor, and that scared me to death.

". . . I suggested that we sing 'O My Father.' I was met with a blank stare. We sang it—it was a terrible cowboy solo. Then I thought, if I could get these people to turn around and kneel by their chairs, they wouldn't be looking at me while I prayed. I asked them if they would and they responded readily. They all knelt down, and I knelt down, and for the second time in my life I talked with God. All fear left me. I didn't worry any more. I was turning it over to him.

"I said to him, among other things, 'Father in Heaven, these folks have left the Church of England. They have come here to-night to hear the truth. You know that I am not prepared to give them what they want, but Thou art, O God, the one that can; and if I can be an instrument through whom You speak, very well, but please take over.'

"When we arose most of them were weeping, as was I. . . . I talked forty-five minutes. I don't know what I said. I didn't talk— God spoke through me. . . . And he spoke so powerfully to that group that at the close of that meeting they came and put their arms around me, held my hands. They said, 'This is what we have been waiting for. Thank God you came.'

"I told you I dragged myself down to that meeting. On my way back home that night I only touched the ground once. . . .

"Within three months every man, woman and child in that audience was baptized a member of the Church . . . and most of them came to Utah and Idaho. I have seen some of them in recent years. They are elderly people now, but they say they never have attended such a meeting, a meeting where God spoke to them."[3]

President Brown's unusual experience well illustrates what can happen if you are prayerful. And Jesus' whole ministry is one illustration after another of life-changing things that can happen to anyone who constantly directs his or her petitions to heaven. So be prayerful—like Jesus.

Chapter Eight

BE PEACEFUL

Jesus said, "Let not your heart be troubled, neither let it be afraid" (John 14:27). We call that manner of speaking a synonymous parallelism: saying the same thing twice. Don't be troubled; don't be afraid.

Given the frightening circumstances of the world around us, how can he say that? How can we be so passive or unresponsive as to not lament the deteriorating conditions in this tumultuous world, where Satan seems to be winning on all sides? The fact is, Satan is not winning on all sides. There is much good in the lives of sincere, God-fearing people everywhere.

For quite some time—for several decades—the Church and the Saints have enjoyed relative quiet and even basked in the praise of the world. The world has seen who we are and what we do, and it has applauded and honored us. But we cannot expect the glow and the adulation to continue indefinitely. "All that will live godly in Christ Jesus shall suffer persecution," Paul wrote to

Timothy (2 Timothy 3:12). In that same chapter Paul describes our day: "This know also, that in the last days perilous times shall come. For men shall be lovers of their own selves [and I am picking out a few key words he uses] . . . unholy . . . without natural affection . . . false accusers . . . fierce . . . despisers of those that are good . . . heady [meaning rash and reckless] . . . highminded . . . lovers of pleasures more than lovers of God . . . led away with divers lusts" (2 Timothy 3:1–6). All of those words accurately describe today's world.

We have known for some time and have been reminded recently that tough times are ahead. I believe we can still live with peace and love and kindness and spirituality and gratitude and all the divine qualities, even as we are surrounded by grossly immoral behavior, terrorism, hate, and persecution. We just have to be calm, as our leaders are calm. How can they, and we, be calm? By seeing "the big picture." We know the end from the beginning. We know that this glorious cause we are fighting for will triumph in the end. We are on the winning team. We just have to make sure we don't ever abandon the team. We stay true through daily, sincere prayer; daily study of God's words; obedience to all the commandments; and especially regular worship in the House of the Lord (which helps us keep all our priorities straight).

Again, I testify that God is a happy Man. I know that because I am a happy man when I have his Spirit with me. You can keep a cheerful face when others around you are despondent. When others appear sad and mad and bad, you can still be glad and peaceful because you know who you are and where you are going, and you have his Spirit with you.

One caution: some might consider it wise to flee the moral and spiritual sicknesses of society and go out into the desert or up into the mountains and isolate and insulate ourselves from all the evils. But the gospel teaches us that unless we are in society's final moments, just before people are destroyed for their total depravity, we are to remain in the social circles in which we have been planted to be a light to others. As our well-used but still relevant cliché says, we must be *in* the world but not *of* the world. Emerson expressed it beautifully: "It is easy in the world to live after the world's opinion; it is easy in solitude to live after our own; but the great man is he who in the midst of the crowd keeps with perfect sweetness the independence of solitude."[1]

The Father, indeed, has great expectations that his chosen children will exercise the true independence of heaven, even while surrounded by wickedness, and still provide for the prodigals a serene view of happy living.

The land where Jesus lived is often called the Holy Land, but today it is not so holy. Jerusalem is called the City of Peace, but there is little peace in that place. Some years ago on a BBC television program with famous Christian theologians, an award-winning Jewish author, Elie Wiesel, commented: "One thing we know. We know when Messiah comes there will be peace; Jesus came, and there is no peace."[2] But what did Jesus say? "Peace I leave with you, *my* peace I give unto you: *not as the world giveth, give I unto you*" (John 14:27; emphasis added).

The Savior promises peace in our lives but not the kind of peace the world is desperate for—the kind of peace that is won at the negotiation table or with heavy armaments on the battlefield.

Scientists inform us that if we could position ourselves right in the center (the eye) of a hurricane, with fierce turbulence all around us, we could sit quietly reading the day's newspaper. It is perfectly calm at the center. So it is with the life of true disciples: though the evils of the world, and even our own saintly trials, rage around us, if we keep the Savior at the center of our lives, we can feel perfect serenity, *his* kind of peace, immediately around us.

Peace is not freedom from conflict or troubles but rather a calm assurance of our good standing before God. The wicked are always agitated, casting up "mire and dirt" like the waters of "the troubled sea" (Isaiah 57:20–21), but the righteous can enjoy serenity, peace, joy, love, spirituality, and all the other desirable virtues even in the midst of the telestial turmoil that seeks to overwhelm us here.

Do not worry, do not be troubled, do not be afraid, he keeps telling us (John 14:1; Joseph Smith–Matthew 1:23; 1 Peter 3:14; D&C 98:18). In him we can have peace no matter what comes. By trusting in him, we are supported and delivered out of all our troubles and fears (Alma 36:3; 38:5). As a bumper sticker reads: "No Jesus, No Peace. Know Jesus, Know Peace."

One day I had a stimulating conversation with my friend Gilbert Sandberg, who was then serving as president of the Guatemala City Guatemala Temple. He philosophized that we should never feel true desperation; in fact, I concluded from our discussion that the word *desperate* shows a lack of faith. Perhaps we should never feel desperate about any event or condition in our life if we really trust Heavenly Father and the Savior—that our life is in their hands, and they know what they are doing with us. We should have confidence in them. Desperation, like doubt, is the antithesis of faith.

Jesus Christ is our Savior not only because he saves us from our sins and weaknesses but also because he saves us from our troubles, our anxieties, our seemingly hopeless moments. He keeps reassuring us, "I will not leave you comfortless. I will come to you" (John 14:18). "These things I have spoken unto you, that in me ye might have peace. In the world ye shall have tribulation: but be of good cheer; I have overcome the world" (John 16:33). He was able to say that in his time period, "in the meridian of time, in the days of wickedness and vengeance" (Moses 7:46). But he has also labeled our day "the last days, . . . the days of wickedness and vengeance" (Moses 7:60). And it is possible to overcome the world in our day also.

You have been specially prepared for these trying days. You have a special dispensation of the grace of God and his calming assurance—his peace—to help you be of good cheer and overcome the world—as Jesus did.

Chapter Nine

BE FRUITFUL

One of the most brilliant and profound outpourings of imagery in all the world's literature is that recorded by John, where Jesus metaphorically calls himself the "true vine" (John 15:1). The analogy manifests perfect knowledge of the details of viticulture—the cultivation of grapes—and of the spiritual life. It implies that there might be other vines to which men could look for sustenance, but Jesus is the only True Vine. The branch that stays firmly connected to the Vine can drink deeply of the Water of Life and absorb the Sun of Righteousness and all other necessary nutrients to assure growth leading to fruitfulness. Despite the pruning (the purging or purifying, meaning the trials of life), or even *because* of such pruning (verse 2), when the branch is cut down (humbled), it can be made more fruitful. Those who remain unproductive will in the end be cut off and burned in the fire (Matthew 7:19; Luke 3:9).

Elder Jeffrey R. Holland taught: "'Abide in me' is an

understandable and beautiful enough concept in the elegant English of the King James Bible, but 'abide' is not a word we use much anymore. So I gained even more appreciation for this admonition from the Lord when I was introduced to the translation of this passage in another language. In Spanish that familiar phrase is rendered *'permaneced en mí.'* Like the English verb 'abide,' *permanecer* means 'to remain, to stay,' but even gringos like me can hear the root cognate there of 'permanence.' The sense of this then is 'stay—but stay *forever.'* That is the call of the gospel message to Chileans and everyone else in the world. Come, but come to remain. Come with conviction and endurance. Come permanently."[1]

"Abide in the vine" (John 15:4) means to remain connected—persist, endure, continue, persevere. All of these action verbs suggest our need to stay close to the Savior. We are totally dependent on him, as sheep are dependent on their shepherd.

Some years ago I took my children a number of times to help a woman operate a petting farm for children in Mapleton, Utah. One day the owner told me that if she ever had to get rid of her animals, she would keep her horses and her sheep. I could understand why she would keep the horses, but I asked her why she would want to keep the dirty, smelly, noisy sheep. She said something I will never forget: "Sheep have a willingness to be dependent."

It took me a while to realize the profound significance of her remark. And I learned why the Good Shepherd has often referred to us as his sheep. He wants us to be dependent upon him. Although there is something to be said for exercising our independence and agency to do a lot of good of our own free will, because the power is in us, yet in another sense we must be dependent on him, for in the end we have absolutely no power to save ourselves. We need his grace and his merits and his atoning sacrifice to change our present fallen condition to something more heavenly. We will never make it without him. Actually, we *cannot* make it without him. We cannot change without him. We are dependent on him.

So it is with this image of the vine. The only way we will be productive or fruitful is to stay attached to our Source of strength and nourishment. "For without me," Jesus warned, "ye can do nothing" (verse 5). Whether in the meridian of time as a fisherman, a publican, or a political zealot, or today as a teacher, a government worker, or a computer consultant, we will all be undistinguished nobodies in the end if we fail to abide in him. We will produce nothing of real, lasting value.

True disciples bring forth much fruit, and thereby they glorify the Father and the Son (verse 8). The Lord does not necessarily require huge, earth-shaking, world-changing accomplishments, but he does expect of us many quiet, unpublicized acts of kindness and compassion.

Why had Jesus taught all these beautiful metaphorical truths? "These things have I spoken unto you, that my joy might remain in you, and that your joy might be full" (verse 11). He is talking to us. If we want to be happy, we must stay close to him and be fruitful, doing all we can to work out our own salvation and helping as many others as possible to do the same. Fruitful means joyful.

Some people these days are concerned not so much about previous generations' fears of disease and death but about their own boredom and lack of entertainment—a worry that they might have time on their hands with nothing to do. A generation has arisen that demands constant, fast-moving stimulation or else boredom sets in—a generation that quickly runs out of things to do.

Contrary to such an attitude, you know that going about doing good, paying attention to the needs of others, and thus helping build the kingdom of God is anything but boring. There is so much good to do, so much encouragement to give, so many burdens to help bear, so many anxieties to help relieve, so many addictions to help overcome, so many people begging for a little loving-kindness that there is no time for languishing in self-pity or wondering what to do next to have fun.

During our service in the lands of Father Lehi, my wife, Marcia, and I noticed that most Guatemalans are short in stature. One day in the cafeteria of the Missionary Training Center, we saw the two custodians standing by one of the beautiful, framed paintings hanging on the walls. The two men were pondering Arnold Friberg's rendering of Alma baptizing in the waters of Mormon. After looking for a few moments at those robust men in the painting, one of the men turned to the other and asked, "What happened to us?"

Sister Ogden and I overheard the question and chuckled, though we knew that some researchers have concluded that the small size of many of the native peoples is related to their lack of good nutrition. As I reflected on that centuries-old question, I

thought about our efforts to help thousands of missionaries prepare to go out and *nourish* the people with the good word of God
so that they too could be fruitful—not just in a temporal way
(though that was important also, and much is being done to provide for Guatemalans' temporal needs) but also in a far-reaching
spiritual way to nurture generations to come.

All of us can blossom where we are planted. Every one of us
knows that there are people all around us who are hurting and
lacking. By praying and being watchful, we can know whom we
can help and how we can help them.

Again, being fruitful is joyful. So go out every day and bring
forth fruit—as Jesus did.

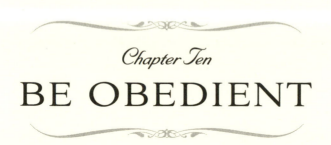

Chapter Ten

BE OBEDIENT

Jesus came to do the will of his Father. Glance down through the following passages from the Gospel of John and notice how obvious that is. There has never been a more loving, adoring relationship between a father and a son in all the universe. And the first law of heaven is obedience:

"I came down from heaven, not to do mine own will, but the will of him that sent me" (John 6:38).

"I do nothing of myself; but as my Father hath taught me. . . . I do always those things that please him" (John 8:28–29).

"Therefore doth my Father love me, because I lay down my life, that I might take it again. . . . This commandment have I received of my Father" (John 10:17–18).

"Even as the Father said unto me, so I speak" (John 12:50).

"The word which ye hear is not mine, but the Father's [who] sent me" (John 14:24).

"That the world may know that I love the Father . . . as the Father gave me commandment, even so I do" (John 14:31).

"As the Father hath loved me, so have I loved you. . . . If ye keep my commandments, ye shall abide in my love; even as I have kept my Father's commandments, and abide in his love" (John 15:9–10).

"I have glorified thee [the Father] on the earth: I have finished the work which thou gavest me to do" (John 17:4).

"The glory which thou gavest me I have given them; that they may be one, even as we are one. . . . That the world may know that thou hast sent me, and hast loved them, as thou hast loved me" (John 17:22–23).

Because Jesus loved his Father, he obeyed him with exactness. I hope each of us is willing to do the same—love the Father and the Savior and obey them with exactness.

We can take the yoke of the Savior's commandments upon us because, as he says, "my yoke is easy and my burden is light" (Matthew 11:30). The word *light* is the opposite of heavy, and it is the opposite of dark. His way is easier, therefore, than the way of the sinner, which is heavy and dark.

Three times in three verses the Lord points out that if we love him, we will keep his commandments (John 14:15, 21, 23). And if we keep his commandments, we can abide in his love continuously (John 15:10). Again, that word *abide* suggests permanence, continuing on forever. *Continuing* is a vital concept in the eternal plan. It is not a good idea to start out on the right path (baptism, activity in the Church, reception of the priesthood and temple ordinances) and then to "fall away into forbidden paths" or "[wander] in strange roads" (1 Nephi 8:28, 32). Some want to follow the Lord and his prophet-leaders when convenient, but when the Lord through his prophet-leaders speaks out in clarion terms against the moral illnesses of our society, they are not sure if they can "continue in the word," or they may be deceived "by the sleight of men, and cunning craftiness, whereby they lie in wait to deceive" (Ephesians 4:14). Some find themselves pitting the words of modern prophets against the words of ancient prophets, or modern scripture against ancient scripture, or the solid words of God against the shaky philosophies of men. "Why call ye me, Lord, Lord, and do not the things which I say?" the Lord asks (Luke 6:46).

On numerous occasions during Jesus' ministry, people received immediate reward for believing and obeying him. To the blind man in Jerusalem, Jesus said, "Go, wash in the pool of Siloam. . . . He went his way therefore, and washed, and came seeing" (John 9:7).

The ten lepers in Samaria were told, "Go shew yourselves unto the priests. And it came to pass, that, as they went, they were cleansed" (Luke 17:14). The scriptures then teach a beautiful lesson about gratitude, with a single Samaritan returning to pour out his deep-felt thanks to the Lord for cleansing him. But back to the first lesson: all then went and obeyed Jesus' instruction, and all were immediately cleansed.

Doctrine and Covenants 82:10 says, "I, the Lord, am bound when ye do 85 percent of what I say . . ." Right? No, of course not. It's really 95 percent. Wrong again. The Lord expects complete obedience—exact and strict obedience. You receive blessings commensurate with your level of obedience. If you almost obey, the Lord almost blesses you! And you get in trouble when you think you are above some commandment, that you are an exception to a rule. Exact obedience is the rule of heaven.

In one of our first classes in the Guatemala MTC, I always told the missionaries that Sister Ogden and I could tell after just a few days who was going to be a great missionary. It was a fairly simple process: future great missionaries were always in the right place at the right time doing the right thing. If it was time to be outside doing exercises or sports, that is what they were doing. If it was time to be in the classroom holding personal scripture study or in their room writing in their journal or a letter home, that is what they were doing. It is a big thing to be dependable, trustworthy, and, as described by two of my favorite words in the Book of Mormon, "firm and steadfast" (1 Nephi 2:10; Helaman 15:8). The missionaries had a great opportunity, a new beginning, in their life right then. For success in the mission and in life, they had to learn to be exactly obedient—always in the right place at the right time doing the right thing.

All of us want to feel secure in these terribly turbulent times. Wouldn't it be wonderful to have God's promise, his *guarantee* of safety in this dangerous world? Well, here is the promised security:

"Whoso would hearken unto the word of God, and would hold fast unto it, they would *never perish;* neither could the temptations and the fiery darts of the adversary overpower them" (1 Nephi 15:24; emphasis added).

So we mortals are all dartboards, and Satan is a professional dart thrower. The fiery darts he is hurling at us these days are pornographic Internet sites, substance abuse, immoral and violent movies, perverted sexual relationships, worldly music, crude and vulgar language, and much more. But the Lord's promise is that the adversary cannot overpower us if we will hold tight to his words, his teachings. "Whoso treasureth up my word, shall not be deceived" (Joseph Smith–Matthew 1:37).

Here is another promise: "It is upon the rock of our Redeemer, who is Christ, the Son of God, that ye must build your foundation; that when the devil shall send forth his mighty winds, yea . . . when all his hail and his mighty storm shall beat upon you, it shall have no power over you to drag you down . . . because of the rock upon which ye are built, which is a sure foundation, a foundation whereon if men build they *cannot fall*" (Helaman 5:12; emphasis added; see also D&C 50:44; 33:13; 6:34).

The promise does not say we *may* not fall or we *probably won't* fall; it says we *cannot* fall if our lives are founded solidly on our Redeemer. That is security!

About the Lord's expectations of us, one teenager wrote:

> *My parents say I must not smoke—*
> *I don't.*
> *Nor listen to a naughty joke—*
> *I don't.*
> *They make it clear: at pretty girls I must not wink*
> *Or ever think about intoxicating drinks—*
> *I don't.*

To tease or flirt is wrong—
  I don't.
I kiss no girl, not even one;
I don't even know how it is done.
You wouldn't think I had much fun—
  I don't!

Parents and leaders are interesting people. When we are young, they impose a lot of rules on us—for our good. Heavenly Father also imposes many rules on us—they are called commandments—for our good. Obedience brings promised blessings. You want a blessing? Obey the law upon which that blessing is predicated, and you get it (D&C 130:21). Guaranteed—though it may be "in his own time, and in his own way, and according to his own will" (D&C 88:68). Nevertheless, the promise is sure. Blessings are inevitable when we are obedient.

Nephi is one of our noblest examples of faith and faithfulness. Look up the last two verses of the book of 1 Nephi; both of those verses contain the words "be obedient" (1 Nephi 22:30–31). Now look up the last words of the book of 2 Nephi, which may well be the last recorded words of that great prophet. Just before the amen you'll notice Nephi's final emphatic words: "I must obey" (2 Nephi 33:15).

So follow Nephi, as he followed the Savior, and follow the Savior, as he followed the Father.

Obey the laws and get the blessings—as Jesus did.

Chapter Eleven

BE LOVING

Faith is the first principle of the gospel. Repentance is the number one doctrine of the kingdom. Obedience is the first law of heaven. And happiness is the object of our existence. But of all things in the gospel, in the scriptures, and in the plan of salvation, that which is *most important* of all is the *love of God.*[1]

In the glorious final chapter of John's Revelation of Jesus Christ, the Beloved Apostle saw the water of life and the tree of life, two prominent images in scripture (Revelation 22:1–2). With the help of the great prophet Nephi, who saw the same imagery more than half a millennium before John, we learn that the water of life and the tree of life both represent the love of God (1 Nephi 11:25), and a major effort of our mortality must be to partake of that water and the fruit of that tree—and to help others to partake also.

Moroni teaches that this love of God is the greatest thing we can possess at the last day (Moroni 7:47). Love is the divine quality we true followers of Jesus should most desire to be filled with, and in that way we will be more like the Savior (Moroni 7:48).

We see in the accounts of Jesus' mortal life that he showed tender, loving feelings toward others. He performed many of his miraculous healings because he felt compassion for the victims of sometimes cruel sicknesses, diseases, and disabilities (Matthew 9:36; 14:14; 20:34; Mark 1:41; 5:19; 6:34; Luke 7:13). He felt their pain—their physical, emotional, mental, and spiritual pain. Frequent expressions of his sensitive recognition of their distress include the phrases "moved with compassion" and "filled with compassion" (Mark 1:41; Matthew 14:14; 3 Nephi 17:6).

One of the moving examples of the Savior's divine quality of love occurred with the passing of his friend Lazarus. When he finally arrived on the outskirts of Bethany, Jesus saw that his dear friends Martha and Mary, sisters of Lazarus, were beside themselves with grief, and he felt it too. Even though he knew that he was going to raise his dead friend back to life, because they hurt, he hurt. Because they wept, he wept. Even those who stood by noticed the grief in Jesus' countenance: "Behold how he loved him!" (John 11:36).

The resurrected Lord dramatically taught a lesson to his chief Apostle, Peter—and through Peter, to us. As they met on the shore of their beloved Sea of Galilee, Jesus directed a penetrating, personal question to Peter: "Lovest thou me?" The answer was genuinely affirmative, of course, but then the instruction came: "Feed my lambs. . . . Feed my sheep" (John 21:15–16). The action verb *feed* in the Greek means to shepherd, tend, care for, or lead. Peter the fisherman was to become Peter the shepherd, tending and caring for the sheep of his Master's fold.

You too are called to feed the flock. Whether it is a large flock (as bishop of a whole ward) or a small flock (as Primary teacher of the Sunbeams)—size does not matter to the Master Shepherd—you are called to watch over, guard, protect, and nourish the sheep under your care. And for the ones who have wandered off, you will search them out and do all you can to guide them back. You don't have to worry about those in other flocks, in other places; you are to care for those over whom you have been given a charge. In other words, you have to *love* them. Jesus was a Rescuer, a Savior, and a Redeemer, and he wants you to become what he is. That is your calling—to be a rescuer, a savior, and a redeemer of those in your flock.

That is what Jesus taught: "Love one another; as I have loved you, that ye also love one another" (John 13:34). The next verse explains that others will know we are his disciples if we have "love one to another."

Later, Jesus said it once again for emphasis: "This is my commandment, That ye love one another, as I have loved you" (John 15:12). Then a third time he said, "These things I command you, that ye love one another" (John 15:17).

One day a friend wrote and asked me to give his son some advice before the young man left on his mission to New York City. Here is what I wrote to that newly called missionary:

"For several days I have thought about what I could say to you that would be of value. I am sure you have heard more than enough already. The mind gets tired and the memory gives up. So

I am going to summarize all you have heard and reduce it to 'easy recall' format.

"Here it is. Are you ready? The best counsel you or anyone else involved in the greatest cause on earth could possibly receive (it is not from me; it is from the One who has universal jurisdiction, who oversees all this work and glory throughout all the 'worlds without number.' It is His counsel). I am giving it to you in just three words. It is all you need:

"LOVE THE PEOPLE!

"Ok, let's break that down into manageable units.

"First and foremost, *love the Father and the Son,* to whose work you are going to dedicate yourself 100 percent. If you really love them, you will obey them; that is, you will obey all the commandments and all the rules.

"Second, *love your companion.* That way, when you teach the people, they will feel the Spirit as it radiates from the two of you, and they may experience true conversion.

"Third, *love the members.* They will help you find and help you teach and convert more people.

"Fourth, *love the New Yorkers.* They are different. They are all different. But they are Heavenly Father's children, and the more you learn to love them, the more you will grow and succeed in this short-term mission, which is part of your whole-life mission.

"Fifth, *love your mission president.* He is one of the main reasons you are going where you are going. He will change your life. Listen to him carefully. Be strictly obedient to what he teaches you, and you will find success.

"Sixth, *love your parents and your family.* Write to them

regularly and share the details of life in the East, but also share some of your innermost feelings, your struggles, your heart-wrenching experiences, and your joys.

"That's it. Simple. Forget all the rest I just wrote to you, and remember three words:

"LOVE THE PEOPLE!"

One more experience. This one was harder.

A few weeks after arriving to preside over the Guatemala MTC, I wrote in my journal:

"We just lost our first missionary. A taxi driver, a friend of the family, came and picked him up to take him home. I've been agonizing over him for eight days, ever since he arrived. He came to me fairly soon after his arrival and told me he didn't want to be here; he didn't want to be a missionary. Talking with him at length, I learned that indeed he was not ready to be a missionary. He had some unresolved problems that made him unworthy to represent the Lord Jesus Christ, though they were problems that he could have resolved here and now if he had wanted to do so. I talked to my contact in the area presidency, who encouraged me to advise the elder's stake president. I did that, and his stake president came to the Training Center and talked with the elder for an hour and a half.

"Day after day, more than once a day, the elder pled with me to make the necessary phone calls to allow him to go home—that he felt uncomfortable here (and didn't want to attend the temple with the other missionaries). I kept putting him off, delaying his departure, hoping that he would experience a change of heart in one of our classes, where the Spirit is so strong. (He was not at all obstructive or rebellious but participated in all class work and personal study and had a good relationship with his companion.) I had such hope for him. After days of his persistence in requesting permission to leave, I finally admitted to him that I had been putting him off, delaying his departure, because I love him, and I couldn't bear to see him abandon the most wonderful thing that has ever come into his life. I just couldn't initiate those final phone calls (to my missionary department contact and a General Authority to approve his departure) because I care about him, and I didn't want to see him suffer remorse for his sad decision. In the end, however, I assured him that we have no desire to *force* anyone to be a missionary, a personal representative of the Lord. He could make the decision, and I would honor it. He made his decision, and he's gone now. I feel to continue to pray for his soul.

"It surprised me how much I came to love this elder and how much it hurt to see him go. There is definitely a mantle of love that comes when one presides.

"Another surprise for me: My heart is not in the ancient ruins. I remember when the call came more than nine years ago to serve in Chile, I was glad in a sense, because I knew if I had been called to a place with lots of fabulous ruins, I might be distracted. But I knew there were few antiquities in Chile that might draw my mind away from the work; I would focus my head and my heart on the people there. Well, here we are in Guatemala, a place with some fabulous ruins all around us, but my heart is not in them. Yes, we will go visit some of the outstanding sites because we have to get out between groups and take a break. But I am not spending all my 'spare time' researching and developing any expertise, even in the Book of Mormon-period remains, because my heart is not there, in all those things. My heart is really going out to the people: I love the *people*.

"People matter more than piles of stone. I feel as Elder LeGrand Richards is reported to have said, when, after sailing across the Sea of Galilee and stepping off the boat at Capernaum and looking around, he exclaimed, 'Where are the people? I didn't come here to see the stones—I came to see the people!'"[2]

People matter. Following Jesus' example, you have to make people the focus of your life. Not *all* people—that was for him and for the prophets and apostles, who are special witnesses of him in all the world. But for you, in your narrow circle, those who come within your sphere of influence are the ones to whom you direct your devoted efforts.

And that is not easy these days. Because of sin, you have a greater challenge than ever before in this increasingly troubled world. As the Savior said, because of iniquity the love of many is waxing cold (Joseph Smith–Matthew 1:30). The world is polarizing; there is a growing contrast between the bad and the good. And the lack of natural affection is spawning unnatural affection.

You are among the good, or you probably wouldn't be reading this book. And the good must get better and better. The harder some people are to love, the more they need your love. Jesus Christ knew that. Joseph Smith knew that. And you too know it is true. There are people out there who need you. So go after them, even those who are straying, and love them—as Jesus does.

Chapter Twelve

BE FORGIVING

A beautiful story of forgiveness is recorded in Luke 7:36–50. When a Pharisee who had invited Jesus to dinner saw a woman giving heartfelt attention to Jesus, he thought to himself that if this man were a prophet, he would know what kind of sinful woman was touching him and would be embarrassed and repulsed by her doing so.

Jesus cut short the Pharisee's condemnatory thoughts by relating a story. "There was a certain creditor which had two debtors: the one owed five hundred pence, and the other fifty. And when they had nothing to pay, he frankly forgave them both. Tell me therefore, which of them will love him most?" Simon the Pharisee replied, "I suppose that he, to whom he forgave most" (verses 41–43). That was the correct answer, but notice how it applied to the current situation.

Extending certain courtesies to an honored guest, such as washing the feet, giving a kiss of greeting, and anointing the head with oil, was customary among the Jews in New Testament times. Jesus chastised the host of this dinner by contrasting Simon's lack of courtesies with the courtesies given him by a sinful woman:

"And he turned to the woman, and said unto Simon, Seest thou this woman? I entered into thine house, thou gavest me no water for my feet: but she hath washed my feet with tears. . . .

"Thou gavest me no kiss: but this woman since the time I came in hath not ceased to kiss my feet. My head with oil thou didst not anoint: but this woman hath anointed my feet with ointment" (verses 44–46).

Jesus continued teaching Simon: "Her sins, which are many, are forgiven" (verse 47). Why? Because she loved much, and she loved much because of her faith in Jesus and in his divine forgiveness. Anyone who has the stains and pains of many sins taken away by the only Person in the entire universe who can take them away is going to love that kind and merciful God. And how are our sins forgiven? Through faith in the Lord Jesus Christ. Faith in him saves us, makes us whole, and brings us peace.

Faith drives us to follow through with the other steps required for forgiveness. We trust that the Savior can and will take away our sins, so we repent of them, and then we experience the baptism of water and the baptism of fire—to wash away and burn out all uncleanliness in us and strengthen us to avoid such sin in the future, which gives us peace.

For Sister Ogden and me, most of our seven hundred days in the Guatemala MTC were full of happy relationships. But there were moments—especially in the first weeks of learning how to deal with many young elders and sisters who still had some frivolous, immature tendencies—that were a bit challenging. The elders were still teenagers, and as someone has suggested, if the Lord had wanted thirty-five-year-old heads on nineteen-year-old bodies, he would have put them there.

One such moment occurred on April 12, 2006, just three months after we arrived in Guatemala. I wrote of the experience in my journal:

"For two or three days, and again today, elders from one of our districts have come to me and criticized another elder or two in the district. Each one who came in for an interview had nothing but bitter accusations and blame to heap on another person. After another such conversation tonight I felt exasperated and at my wits' end, wondering what to do. If I didn't do something, and soon, several elders could be wanting to quit the mission and return home—feeling that all this bickering and contention couldn't be what they had sacrificed to come for. I trusted an impression I had, and I called the ten elders together into one room.

"I told them that I have not had such a terrible experience in three months here. I could not believe how much criticism and accusation and blame I was hearing, and how immature it all was. I was embarrassed and ashamed at what I saw happening. And I told them I knew where it was all coming from. I knew that Satan was trying to destroy the Spirit among these new servants of the Lord. I said to the ten elders that we needed to kneel together and pray for help. I asked one elder to pray, and by the time he had finished his pleading with Heavenly Father to forgive everyone in the room, the elders were all sobbing—some of them almost uncontrollably.

"After that elder prayed, I asked if another one felt like praying. The second one poured out his heart to Heavenly Father. Four others followed. After all the prayers, I asked if anyone wanted to say anything to another in the group. Several proceeded to ask forgiveness of someone else, still through lots of tears. In just a few minutes a remarkable Spirit had come over the whole group. After a while I asked them if they all felt what had just happened in that room. They all had. There had been a depressingly negative feeling to begin with, but when the Spirit of the Lord took over the room, such a feeling of peace and love and forgiveness enveloped us. I pled with them to never forget that moment. Here we are learning the gospel of Jesus Christ, and we just learned in the most dramatic way I have seen for a long time how to use the gospel we are going out to preach.

"I learned something wonderful tonight. At first I really felt like the burden was on my shoulders to find a solution to all this friction, but the thought of trying to resolve these situations all by myself is overwhelming and frightening. I don't need to. It is the Lord's work, not mine. I just need to turn to him and his Spirit to change some hearts. Few times in my life have I witnessed such a thing as I saw tonight."[1]

In Doctrine and Covenants 64, our Savior says, "I, the Lord, forgive sins [those first five words are absolutely wonderful] unto those who confess their sins before me and ask forgiveness" (verse 7).

Then he adds some pointed warning words about what happened to some former-day Saints: "My disciples, in days of old, sought occasion against one another and forgave not one another in their hearts; and for this evil they were afflicted and sorely chastened" (verse 8). Some of the fiery trials and painful ordeals they passed through they brought on themselves by their own shameful misbehavior and hard-heartedness.

Then Jesus teaches the divine lesson: "Wherefore, I say unto you, that ye ought to forgive one another; for he that forgiveth not his brother his trespasses standeth condemned before the Lord; for there remaineth in him the greater sin. I, the Lord, will forgive whom I will forgive, but of you it is required to forgive all men" (verses 9–10).

But there are tragically difficult offenses and sins against us these days, such as physical, emotional, and spiritual abuse among family members and even Church members. How can we simply pardon someone who has done unspeakable harm and inflicted lasting damage? Actually, we cannot do it alone; but by calling on the powers of heaven and drawing strength from the incomparable gift of the Holy Ghost, we can do as Jesus did, withholding judgment, rising above the sin of the sinner, and showing Christlike loving-kindness, mercy, and forgiveness.

Sometimes we understand the gospel principle and would like to live it, but what happened was too painful; there is still too much hurt. "I know I need to forgive him," you say, "and I really want to, but I just can't do it. I cannot forgive him." Jesus' warning is sobering. If you don't forgive, there remains in you the greater sin. But you retort, "Wait a minute. He's the one who sinned. I'm the victim! How can I be held accountable for a 'greater sin'?"

The reason you are in a worse position is that you are trying to be like Jesus, and forgiving is divine. Forgiving is learning divine love. And that is what you yourself want on the great Day of Judgment: his mercy, his kindness, his love, and his forgiveness. Do unto others as you would have him do unto you.

Notice one detail in verse 8: disciples back in days of old refused to forgive one another *"in their hearts"* (emphasis added). It is fairly easy to use our mouths and say, "I'm sorry," but sometimes words are cheap. The Savior requires us to forgive more deeply, in our hearts.

Can you really expect Heavenly Father to forgive you of all your sins if you are holding out and refuse to forgive others? The everlasting gospel teaches that to be forgiven, you must forgive. The Prophet Joseph Smith showed you how you can do it. He once remarked that "all was well between him and the heavens; that he had no enmity against any one; and as the prayer of Jesus, or his pattern, so prayed Joseph—'Father, forgive me my trespasses as I forgive those who trespass against me,' for I freely forgive all men. If we would secure and cultivate the love of others, we must love others, even our enemies as well as friends."[2]

President Joseph F. Smith added: "It is extremely hurtful for any man holding the Priesthood, and enjoying the gift of the Holy Ghost, to harbor a spirit of envy, or malice, or retaliation, or intolerance toward or against his fellowmen. We ought to say in our hearts, let God judge between me and thee, but as for me, I will forgive. I want to say to you that Latter-day Saints who harbor a feeling of unforgiveness in their souls are more guilty and more censurable than the one who has sinned against them. Go home and dismiss envy and hatred from your hearts; dismiss the feeling of unforgiveness; and cultivate in your souls that spirit of Christ which cried out upon the cross, 'Father, forgive them; for they know not what they do.' This is the spirit that Latter-day Saints ought to possess all the day long. The man who has that spirit in his heart and keeps it there will never have any trouble with his neighbor."[3]

If you are bitten by a rattlesnake, you don't run after the rattlesnake to strike back at it; you *get the venom out of you* so it won't destroy you.

If strained relations or friction exist between you and anyone else, before going to the temple or to sacrament meeting and renewing covenants with God, first be reconciled with that person—talk things over, work it out, resolve differences, forgive and forget. "If thy brother shall trespass against thee, go and tell him his fault between thee and him alone: if he shall hear thee, thou hast gained thy brother" (Matthew 18:15). Then you can approach the Lord and his sacred things with full purpose of heart and, as he says, "I will receive you" (3 Nephi 12:24).

You know in this very moment if there is someone with whom you have a strained relationship, against whom you have hard feelings. The law of the gospel requires you to go to that person now and work things out. What gets in the way of doing that? Pride, of course. *That person* has too much pride. (It seems it is always the other person's fault.) But, you say, it really is *his* fault. You are stubborn, and you are waiting for the person to come to you. The law of the gospel requires you to humble yourself and go to that person—even if that person really is the party more responsible for the offense—and ask for forgiveness and resolution of the conflict.

When a person goes meekly and sincerely to seek forgiveness of another, by accepting at least part of the responsibility for the discord, usually—though not always—the other person's heart will soften, and the person will also admit to some responsibility and desire to work things out. If the other person does not soften but remains hard and continues hostile, at least you have done your part and made things right in your own heart.

In a thought-provoking article titled "Bitterness Leads to Shorter Life," Dr. Robert Jay Rowen writes: "To err is human; to forgive is divine. That old adage is now being confirmed in modern research. In a study conducted by survey and published in the *Journal of Adult Development* (2001; 8:249–257), great benefits, including greater longevity, were seen in those who professed an ability to forgive. . . .

"Younger adults (18–44) were less likely to forgive others than middle age (45–64) or older adults (over 65). Young adults who reported high levels of self-forgiveness were more likely to be satisfied with their lives, while middle age and older adults who were able to forgive others were more likely to report increased life satisfaction. Attendance at religious service was associated with better stress scores, improved life satisfaction, and better self-health ratings.

"I, for one, believe forgiveness is the most divine of all human attributes. Asking for forgiveness is the first step, but granting forgiveness is the most important. These actions wipe the slate clean, for both the perpetrator and the victim.

"To ask for or grant forgiveness does not mean to avoid responsibility for the consequences of the actions. The greatest forgiveness comes with the perpetrator making proper restitution, thus putting true repentance into physical form.

"I strongly encourage all my chronically ill patients to immediately forgive everyone for everything that may have ever been done to them. Taking ANY bitterness to the grave does no one any good, especially the one holding on to it. Better to let go, unconditionally forgive, and love. Freeing those pent-up emotions is one less burden for your body to carry, especially when it's seeking to rid itself of disease."[4]

Perhaps the two greatest requirements in the gospel are to repent and to forgive. A happy marriage, for example, is the union between two good forgivers. Joseph Smith told the original Relief Society sisters:

"Nothing is so much calculated to lead people to forsake sin as to take them by the hand, and watch over them with tenderness. When persons manifest the least kindness and love to me, O what power it has over my mind, while the opposite course has a tendency to harrow up all the harsh feelings and depress the human mind. . . . The nearer we get to our heavenly Father, the more we are disposed to look with compassion on perishing souls; we feel that we want to take them upon our shoulders, and cast their sins behind our backs."[5]

Complete forgiveness for all our little failings and all our outright sins is what we hope to receive from the Savior. You have frequent opportunities while here in mortality to learn to be like him, and one of the most important godly qualities you can learn is to forgive—as Jesus does.

Chapter Thirteen

BE LONG-SUFFERING

You were not sent away from your heavenly home to go through this brief schooling, training, and testing experience to be comfortable but rather to be challenged. You knew things were going to get complicated. Even Jesus' life was going to be complicated—and painful. "Yet," as the scripture says, "learned he obedience by the things which he suffered" (Hebrews 5:8).

Remember the beautiful lessons from the vine back in chapter 9, "Be Fruitful"? Jesus is the Vine, and he explained that "every branch," even *the* Branch, "that beareth fruit, he [the Father] purgeth it, that it may bring forth more fruit" (John 15:2). The purging tests, tries, proves, and purifies. And some of those tests and trials can really hurt.

Pottery can be beautiful and impress with potential, but it has to go through the fire. Not all vessels make it; some crack, break, and crumble. There is adversity and pain in our lives to make us tougher. The Lord *tenderizes* us by pounding on us to humble us and make us more spiritually productive.

"If the world hate you, ye know that it hated me before it hated you. . . . The servant is not greater than his lord. If they have persecuted me, they will also persecute you" (John 15:18, 20). "Ye shall weep and lament . . . and ye shall be sorrowful, but your sorrow shall be turned into joy. . . . And ye now therefore have sorrow: but I will see you again, and your heart shall rejoice, and your joy no man taketh from you" (John 16:20, 22).

Jesus was criticized, belittled, mocked, spit upon, slapped, and knocked around (see, for example, John 18:22), but he was gentle under provocation. He had indeed overcome the world.

The two disciples walking the road to Emmaus with the un-recognized resurrected Savior were chastened by him and educated by him on the grand purpose of his life: "Ought not Christ to have suffered these things, and to enter into his glory?" (Luke 24:26).

Jesus is our Exemplar in all things. His crown of thorns came first, and then came his crown of glory. There seems to be an eternal principle in operation. Think about the lesson in the following passages:

"My joy cometh over them after wading through much affliction and sorrow" (Alma 7:5).

"Bear with patience thine afflictions, and I will give unto you success" (Alma 26:27).

"This is the account of . . . their sufferings in the land, their sorrows, and their afflictions, and their incomprehensible joy" (Alma 28:8).

"After much tribulation come the blessings" (D&C 58:4).

"Thine adversity and thine afflictions shall be but a small moment; and then, if thou endure it well, God shall exalt thee on high" (D&C 121:7–8).

It is pretty clear, isn't it? The eternal equation operating here is that *after* affliction, sorrow, long-suffering, tribulation, and adversity, *then* come joy, success, blessings, and exaltation.

Can we be grateful for pain, suffering, affliction, and conflict in our lives?

Are we not grateful for the ordeals Joseph of old went through (sold by his brothers, falsely accused, and unjustly imprisoned) to save the covenant people?

Are we not grateful for the torturous pain Jesus went through to atone for our sins?

Are we not grateful for the confusion in young Joseph Smith's mind that led, despite intervening persecution, to the restoration of the Church and the fulness of the gospel?

Are we not grateful for the physical trials of Brigham Young and thousands of righteous people for persevering in establishing the headquarters of the Church in the Rocky Mountains?

The lesson is that much good can result from hardship and suffering.

For the next several minutes you can have an absolutely inspiring meeting with the Holy Spirit if you will prayerfully read and ponder the following quotations from great people who knew trials and afflictions and who understood the eternally valuable lessons that come from them.

The Prophet Joseph Smith:

"Inasmuch as God hath said that He would have a tried people, that He would purge them as gold, now we think that this time He has chosen His own crucible, wherein we have been tried; and we think if we get through with any degree of safety, and shall have kept the faith, that it will be a sign to this generation, altogether sufficient to leave them without excuse; and we think also, it will be a trial of our faith equal to that of Abraham, and that the ancients will not have whereof to boast over us in the day of judgment, as being called to pass through heavier afflictions; that we may hold an even weight in the balance with them."[1]

President Brigham Young:

"All intelligent beings who are crowned with crowns of glory, immortality, and eternal lives must pass through every ordeal appointed for intelligent beings to pass through, to gain their glory and exaltation. Every calamity that can come upon mortal beings will be suffered to come upon the few, to prepare them to enjoy the presence of the Lord. If we obtain the glory that Abraham obtained, we must do so by the same means that he did. If we are ever prepared to enjoy the society of Enoch, Noah, Melchizedek, Abraham, Isaac, and Jacob, or of their faithful children, and of the faithful Prophets and Apostles, we must pass through the same experience, and gain the knowledge, intelligence, and endowments that will prepare us to enter into the celestial kingdom of our Father and God. How many of the Latter-day Saints will endure all these things, and be prepared to enjoy the presence of the Father and the Son? You can answer that question at your leisure. Every trial and experience you have passed through is necessary for your salvation."[2]

"It is recorded that Jesus was made perfect through suffering. If he was made perfect through suffering, why should we imagine for one moment that we can be prepared to enter into the kingdom of rest with him and the Father, without passing through similar ordeals?"[3]

President John Taylor:

"I heard the Prophet Joseph say . . . on one occasion: 'You will have all kinds of trials to pass through. And it is quite as necessary for you to be tried as it was for Abraham and other men of God, and . . . God will feel after you, and He will take hold of you and wrench your very heart strings, and if you cannot stand it you will not be fit for an inheritance in the Celestial Kingdom of God.'"[4]

President George Q. Cannon:

"Every Latter-day Saint who gains a celestial glory will be tried to the very uttermost. If there is a point in our character that is weak and tender, you may depend upon it that the Lord will reach after that, and we will be tried at that spot[,] for the Lord will test us to the utmost before we can get through and receive that glory and exaltation which He has in store for us as a people."[5]

Elder Orson F. Whitney:

"No pain that we suffer, no trial that we experience is wasted. It ministers to our education, to the development of such qualities as patience, faith, fortitude and humility. All that we suffer and all that we endure, especially when we endure it patiently, builds up our characters, purifies our hearts, expands our souls, and makes us more tender and charitable, more worthy to be called the children of God . . . and it is through sorrow and suffering, toil and tribulation, that we gain the education that we come here to acquire and which will make us more like our Father and Mother in heaven."[6]

President Spencer W. Kimball:

"Being human, we would expel from our lives physical pain and mental anguish and assure ourselves of continual ease and comfort, but if we were to close the doors upon sorrow and distress, we might be excluding our greatest friends and benefactors. Suffering can make saints of people as they learn patience, long-suffering, and self-mastery."[7]

President Boyd K. Packer:

"Some are tested by poor health, some by a body that is deformed or homely. Others are tested by handsome and healthy bodies; some by the passion of youth; others by the erosions of age. Some suffer disappointment in marriage, family problems; others live in poverty and obscurity. Some (perhaps this is the hardest test) find ease and luxury.

"All are part of the test, *and there is more equality in this testing than sometimes we suspect.*"[8]

Elder Neal A. Maxwell:

"How can you and I really expect to glide naively through

life, as if to say, 'Lord, give me experience, but not grief, not sorrow, not pain, not opposition, not betrayal, and certainly not to be forsaken. Keep from me, Lord, all those experiences which made Thee what Thou art! Then let me come and dwell with Thee and fully share Thy joy!'"[9]

One of my favorite paintings is *When the Angels Come,* by Clark Kelley Price. Following is the artist's poignant description of the subject of the painting:

"The story behind it comes from an address by President David O. McKay given at an annual Relief Society conference in 1947.

"In that address, President McKay talked of the criticism given by a teacher who commented to his class that it was very unwise to have even permitted the Saints to cross the plains under such circumstances as did the Willie and Martin Handcart Companies. President McKay said:

"'Some sharp criticism of the Church and its leaders was being indulged in for permitting any company of converts to venture across the plains with no more supplies or protection than a handcart caravan afforded.

"'An old man [Francis Webster] in the corner sat silent and listened as long as he could stand it, then he arose and said things that no person who heard him will ever forget. His face was white with emotion, yet he spoke calmly, deliberately, but with great earnestness and sincerity.

"'In substance [he] said, "I ask you to stop this criticism. You are discussing a matter you know nothing about. Cold historic facts mean nothing here, for they give no proper interpretation of the questions involved. Mistake to send the handcart company out so late in the season? Yes. But I was in that company and my wife was in it. . . . We suffered beyond anything you can imagine, and many died of exposure and starvation, but . . . [we] came through with the absolute knowledge that God lives, for *we became acquainted with him in our extremities.*

""'I have pulled my handcart when I was so weak and weary from illness and lack of food that I could hardly put one foot ahead of the other. I have looked ahead and seen a patch of sand or a hill slope, and I have said, I can go only that far and there I must give up, for I cannot pull the load through it. I have gone on to that sand and when I reached it, the cart began pushing me. I have looked back many times to see who was pushing my cart, but my eyes saw no one. I knew then that the angels of God were there.

""'Was I sorry that I chose to come by handcart? No. Neither then nor any minute of my life since. The price we paid to become acquainted with God was a privilege to pay, and I am thankful that I was privileged to come in the Martin handcart company.""" [10]

Expanding on the principles in that emotional story, President James E. Faust explained that "it is part of the purging toll exacted of some to become acquainted with God. In the agonies of life, we seem to listen better to the faint, godly whisperings of the Divine Shepherd." [11]

President Marion G. Romney expounded on the value of the hard lessons of life: "I have seen the remorse and despair in the lives of men who, in the hour of trial, have cursed God and died spiritually. And I have seen people rise to great heights from what seemed to be unbearable burdens.

"Finally, I have sought the Lord in my own extremities and learned for myself that my soul has made its greatest growth as I have been driven to my knees by adversity and affliction."[12]

Just as gold is smelted in the fire to remove impurities, so God tries his people with fire to remove impurities. The Lord is working hard to draw impurities out of you. Just as a diamond is carefully faceted and polished to reveal its inner beauty, so you are shaped and polished. Trials are not punishment inflicted by a vengeful God but are tests by a loving Father who wants you to be refined and polished. Your impurities, weaknesses, and faults get burned away *if* you can withstand the heat and the pressure of your trials. Refineries heat up the metal to its melting point, at which time the impurities separate. In a similar way, God turns up the heat until you reach the point that you become refined so you can be of greater use to him. The temperature necessary to refine each of us is different. Refinement is customized for each of us by a perfect and omniscient Father. It helps to know that troubles and trials are purposeful; you endure them for good reasons. Knowing that fact helps you to suffer long and endure well.

Life is a contact sport! In the end, God will look you over not for medals, awards, or diplomas but for scars. One of my New Testament students wrote to me:

"I am reminded about how the Lord taught that a man sits down before he builds a house and considers the cost. We shouldn't be surprised that a big house with extra comforts and accessories will be expensive—in the same sense that eternal life is 'expensive.' To obtain our mansion with the Lord, the cost must be outrageous. Yes, Christ's Atonement is paying for a lot of it, but should we be surprised that it costs a lot? It's hard. Where much is given much is required. I like the Spanish verb used in this concept. When I return to heaven and someone asks me how life was, I will reply in Spanish: *'Me costó mucho, pero valió la pena!'* [It cost me a lot, but it was worth the pain!]"

The Spanish phrase *vale la pena* fascinates me. It can be translated "It's worth it." The literal translation, however, is "It's worth the pain." That translation prompts me to ponder the tribulation that comes to one and all in this life. The difficulties, challenges, trials, hardships, setbacks, afflictions, and sufferings are all purposeful; they can be painful, but they are "worth the pain." The hardest lessons usually teach you the most; they are fire that burns the dross out of you, purifying and refining you. Heavenly Father knows what he is doing with you when he sends the fiery trials. In the end you will see that they are worth the pain you suffered. You certainly will be forever grateful for the pain the Savior suffered, and you will eternally recognize the worth of that pain.

We are reflecting here on the concept of *long-suffering*. To summarize, it will help to define this virtue and describe, in practical ways, how to acquire it.

Long-suffering means you are slow to anger, not easily provoked. You avoid becoming upset, negative, critical, sarcastic, and condemnatory. You don't make hasty, spur-of-the-moment comments that leave you with regrets, wishing you had not said them. You do not envy others, and you are not selfish. Long-suffering also means that you are willing to endure all things, including an infinite variety of trials. When you are sick or in pain or extremely tired, it is harder to control your emotions, and you more readily react negatively. Trials may also include challenges with mental health, which are not among the so-called "noble" trials. When you have a broken bone or diabetes or leukemia or some other kind of cancer, you receive deserved sympathy, but when you suffer from any of numerous kinds of chemical imbalances and mental ailments—such as depression or bipolar disorder—it is harder for others to accept and understand what you are experiencing. Trials may also include being unable to have children or having a rebellious child or an unfaithful spouse or a loved one with a destructive addiction or an abusive acquaintance. All these trials and many others require a long-suffering nature. God himself is long-suffering, and he wants you to become as he is.

How do you acquire this divine quality of being long-suffering? The Holy Ghost instills it in you. If you have the Spirit of the Lord, you will be long-suffering. And how do you get the Spirit? Through obedience to God's commandments and especially through sincere daily prayer and searching of the scriptures. You receive the Spirit best when you are focused on other people—loving them by serving them.

So go ahead and suffer long, endure the trials, and endure them well—as Jesus did.

Chapter Fourteen

BE PERSEVERING

Have you ever noticed that sometimes the most glorious and elevated experiences of life are preceded or followed by the most negative and depressing experiences of life? Welcome to mortality! That's the way life seems to go—just when you are enjoying something exquisitely spiritual, along comes something terribly disheartening. Or vice versa—you have sunk to the depths, but because you faithfully persevere, something occurs that raises you to the heavens.

Looking back through sacred history, you can see a host of striking examples of this phenomenon:

In the Sacred Grove the darkness of the destructive powers of Satan overpowered the boy Joseph, but the brilliant appearance of Gods immediately dispersed the darkness.

In the John Johnson farmhouse, a vision of the degrees of glory (recorded in Doctrine and Covenants 76) was given to Joseph Smith. That revelation is one of the greatest ever entrusted to man, "a transcript from the records of the eternal world . . . [of which] every honest man is constrained to exclaim: 'It came from God.'"[1] But soon after that glorious connection with heaven came the brutal tar-and-feathering of the Prophet, which could be called "a transcript from the records of the fiends of hell of which every honest man is constrained to exclaim: 'It came from the devil.'"

In Kirtland an extraordinary spiritual outpouring was experienced at the dedication of the temple there, but not many months later apostasy raised its ugly head, and murderous sentiments forced the Prophet to flee.

Eighteen hundred years earlier at the foot of the Mount of Olives, the Savior descended below all things as he suffered the incomprehensible burden of the sins of the world. A short time later, from the same Mount of Olives, he ascended above all things as he and his disciples exulted in the climaxing moments of his mortal ministry.

At Golgotha the Savior endured horrible pain and torture, shedding his blood on the cross for the sins of humankind. But then from the garden sepulcher, he raised his body to living immortality and the permanent joy of eternal life.

Two of our greatest examples to emulate, the Lord of our Salvation and the Prophet of the Restoration, are superb illustrations of lives full of contrasts and contradictions, requiring corresponding perseverance. Andrew C. Skinner wrote: "Gethsemane was the bitterest anguish, the greatest contradiction, the gravest injustice. Irony and contradiction are two of the best descriptors of Gethsemane's bitter cup, causing thoughtful disciples to reflect

Happy like Jesus

on the nature of tests and trials in mortality. By studying the bitter cup, we can see how the bitterest agony for One opened the door to the sweetest ecstasy for all. The Prophet Joseph Smith taught that the Savior 'descended in suffering below that which man can suffer; or, in other words, suffered greater sufferings, and was exposed to more powerful contradictions than any man can be' (*Lectures on Faith*, 5:2). Perhaps the greatest trials are those that seem the most unfair, but the faithful may take comfort in knowing that there is One who understands with perfect empathy. Elder Neal A. Maxwell said of the Savior: 'At the end, meek and lowly Jesus partook of the most bitter cup without becoming the least bitter' (*Ensign*, May 1989, 63).

"Perhaps it was the night of infinite suffering *because* of infinite contradiction. Though Jesus was the Son of the Highest, in Gethsemane he descended below all things. Though he was sent out of love (John 3:16) and though he was characterized as the embodiment of love (1 John 4:8), in Gethsemane he was surrounded by hate and betrayal. Though he was the light and life of the world, in Gethsemane he was subjected to darkness and spiritual death. Though he was sinless, in Gethsemane he was weighed down by monumental sin and iniquity. Though he gave no offense in anything (2 Corinthians 6:3), in Gethsemane he suffered for the offenses of all. In Gethsemane, the sinless One became the great sinner (2 Corinthians 5:21), that is, he experienced fully the plight of sinners. Though he was fully deserving of the Father's love and the Father's glory, in Gethsemane he suffered the wrath of Almighty God.

"Because the Savior endured perfectly his staggering

contradictions, we will be recompensed for our own faithful endurance of life's contradictions, injustices, and flat-out unfair circumstances. That is, through the Atonement, all of life's contradictions, all injustices, and all unfair circumstances will be made up to us; they will all be put right—if we remain faithful to the Savior.

"We, like Jesus, suffer contradictions as part of our probation on this earth. It is what we do in the face of those contradictions, how we react, that demonstrates our commitment to God and thus determines our place in eternity. The greater the contradiction, faithfully endured, the greater the blessing enjoyed afterward."[2]

During recent years Sister Ogden and I have experienced some trials too sensitive to talk about. They have been our Zion's Camp, involving the lowest of trying lows and the highest of sacred highs. The Savior, the Master Teacher, has taught us. As he burns away the dross from us in the furnace of affliction, the burning or cleansing is painful but purifying.

This matter of heart-wrenching contradictions is a refining principle, very much related to the subject of the previous chapter—long-suffering. The contradictions are really incongruities, things happening that seem so out of place with the righteous life we are trying to live—inconsistent, inappropriate, improper for the noble destiny we are trying to pursue.

Talk with Joseph of Egypt about the contradictions of life. Or talk with Joseph of New York, Ohio, Missouri, and Illinois about the incongruities of life. Or better yet, talk with Jesus of Nazareth about the incongruities and contradictions of his exalted mission. Are we better than any of them?

As the saying goes, life is what happens to you while you are making other plans. Heavenly Father and the Savior know perfectly well what each of us needs by way of preparatory lessons for eternity. Some of our earthly experiences are definitely going to challenge us and cause us high anxiety and deep anguish; each of us gets our very own crucible in which we are tested to the core. It is all purposeful. The greatest lessons come at a high price.

In the last days the Lord has repeated his eternal truth: "After much tribulation come the blessings" (D&C 58:4). Woes of all kinds have been prophesied—economic, physical, political, medical, sociological, moral, and especially spiritual—and all of these are both national and personal. But they will be followed by the resolution of all conflicts and the removal of all evils. After all the contradictions of life and trials of our faith come the most glorious conditions, surpassing Eden.

We have been taught by the best examples how to persevere, so we just need to do it—like Jesus.

Chapter Fifteen

BE UNITED

Jesus prayed for the Apostles and for all those who believed in him through their teaching that they might be one, that they might be united. Why? So "the world may believe that thou [the Father] hast sent me" (John 17:21; see also verse 23).

The concept of oneness is important and urgent in the gospel of Jesus Christ. It is the quintessential message inherent in the otherwise abstract English word *atonement* ("at-*one*-ment"). It is the idea of becoming one, the same message suggested by the Latin words inscribed on United States currency: *E pluribus unum,* meaning "out of many, one."

Note how the scriptures use various parts of the Father's crowning creation, the physical body of his children, to illustrate the desirability of oneness: the children of God looked "forward with *one eye,* . . . having their *hearts knit together* in unity" (Mosiah 18:21; emphasis added); "them that believed were of *one heart* and of *one soul*" (Acts 4:32; emphasis added); "his people

Zion . . . were of *one heart* and *one mind*" (Moses 7:18; emphasis added); "we, being many, are *one body* in Christ" (Romans 12:5; emphasis added); "stand fast in *one spirit,* with *one mind*" (Philippians 1:27; emphasis added).

One eye, one mind, one heart, one body, one spirit, and one soul—every member of the body is needed; all members must unite for the body of Christ to function perfectly. "There is neither Jew nor Greek," Paul wrote, "for ye are *all one* in Christ" (Galatians 3:28; emphasis added). And, we might add, there is neither European nor Asian nor African nor North American nor Latin American in the Church; all are citizens of the kingdom of God.

To establish Zion, then, we must become of one heart and one mind. God seems to be celebrating unity, not diversity. That may not be too popular a notion in the world, but the Godhead is encouraging us to become as they are—to feel and to think as they do.

And where are we more united, as one, than any other place? In the house of God. In his holy temple we present ourselves equally before the Lord, all dressed in the same white clothing symbolic of cleanliness and purity. No one is better than anyone else. No matter how much money we possess, what executive position we have, or what Church position we serve in, all are alike before God. All ordinances of the temple unite us, helping us to become one.

"I and my father are one," Jesus proclaimed (John 10:30; see also D&C 50:43; 93:3). And John testified that "there are three that bear record in heaven, the Father, the Word, and the Holy

Ghost: and *these three are one*" (1 John 5:7; emphasis added). So much alike are they that if we know one, we know the others. The Father, the Son, and the Holy Ghost are "*one God*" (2 Nephi 31:21; emphasis added; see also Alma 11:44; 3 Nephi 11:36; D&C 20:28).

Of us the Savior said, "They may become the sons of God, even one in me as I am one in the Father, as the Father is one in me, that *we may be one*" (D&C 35:2; emphasis added).

Is all this "three are one" merely theological double-talk, or is there something profoundly significant and sacred in this doctrine?

Surely the three Gods are teaching us mortals the fundamental and indispensable principle that will lead us to become as they are. In his great Intercessory Prayer, Jesus, our Advocate with the Father, pleaded: "Holy Father, keep . . . those whom thou hast given me, that they may be one, as we are" (John 17:11). "That they *all may be one;* as thou, Father, art in me, and I in thee, that they also may *be one in us. . . .* And the glory which thou gavest me I have given them; *that they may be one, even as we are one:* I in them, and thou in me, that they may be *made perfect in one*" (John 17:21–23; emphasis added).

That is the foundational reason for us to be united as one: to become perfect. That is the preparation required for our great *re-union,* becoming one again. "I say unto you, *be one;* and if ye are not one ye are not mine" (D&C 38:27; emphasis added).

In all these passages we see the basic meaning of that otherwise abstract word *atonement:* the great sacrificial offering of the

Lamb is meant to help us become as one with him and the Father and as one with each other.

I worked with David Galbraith for many years in the Holy Land, and we taught together at Brigham Young University. In the mid-1990s I served as his counselor in a BYU stake presidency. President Galbraith prayed for each of us stake leaders by name. One day in the Provo Utah Temple, he received a revelation directed to us:

"Glorify your wife! Praise her. Exalt her in the eyes of others. Then she will empower you, magnify you, honor you, and exalt you. You will be a greater blessing to each other. This is a sacred key to happiness—found with your wife in the temple. If things are right with your companion, things will go right in your life. You will have more charity. Your relationship is forever. Grow together, and don't let either one get ahead of or behind the other spiritually."

So here is one specific relationship—our most important mortal relationship of husband and wife—in which we can practice the principle of being united. If the two of us cannot arrive at a good working relationship here in this temporal probation, this testing ground of essential relationships, what is the likelihood that we would want to be living and working together for all eternity?

Sister Ogden is funny. She has noticed changes in her physical body as she ages. One day during our three-year residence in Santiago, Chile, she wrote:

"Joseph [our younger son] keeps kidding me about my saggy, baggy body and all the wrinkles I am getting as I get older. One day I laughed and told him that as my mortal body gets older and baggier, my spirit was getting more glamorous, more sophisticated, and more stunning. I told him that in a few years this baggy body would be put six feet under, allowing my gorgeous spirit to rise up free of the old body. And the reason my spirit is becoming so beautiful, glamorous, sophisticated, and buff is because it gets daily exercise as I read the scriptures and sacrifice my time serving in the Church and serving my family. It gets a spiritual workout that far exceeds Jane Fonda's daily three hours. My spirit is becoming a real knockout."[1]

Some years later in Guatemala City, she wrote:

"I was putting on some make-up the other day, thinking how much I had aged here. I suddenly realized that I now no longer look like the person I really am and will be forever. And it is only going to get worse. The real me will not emerge until I die. My grandchildren will think of me forever as old, just like I think of my grandmother only in terms of old."[2]

After hearing about that observation from Sister Ogden, David Galbraith took up the theme once again about exalting our wives. He wrote to me, quoting Elder James E. Talmage:

"'Mortal eye cannot see nor mind comprehend the beauty, glory, and majesty of a righteous woman made perfect in the celestial kingdom of God. . . . [There] shall woman reign by Divine right, a queen in the resplendent realm of her glorified state, even as exalted man shall stand, priest and king unto the Most High God.'"[3]

"My wife, too, reminds me of what a beauty queen she will be, both physically and spiritually, in her resurrected state without all the telestial fat. Let's hope we men make it. There will be a lot of jealous guys when they see our wives.

"One more thought. A mission, where we serve together, teaches us how to 'rule and reign' together. Most couples in this mortal experience don't learn that.

"The patriarchal order is a condition where woman shares with man the blessings of the Priesthood, where husband and wife minister, as Elder Talmage wrote, 'seeing and understanding alike, and cooperating to the full in the government of their family kingdom.'[4]

"In all our professional lives we have never learned that sacred principle, but one of the single greatest lessons we learn on a mission together is how to see and understand alike and cooperate. Looking at these missions in a selfish way, they are more for our spiritual progress as husband and wife than for other things we do."[5]

There is something to be said for the true independence of heaven and using our diverse personalities and abilities to build the kingdom of God and our own family-kingdom in our individual ways. The principle of unity is likewise vital and indispensable to perpetuate the everlasting plan of God.

You and I must be united in thought and action with the Gods, and we must be united with one another to make the kingdom flourish, especially in family relationships between husband and wife. We must come to see eye to eye and become as one in our most important thoughts and feelings—just as the Father and the Son are one in their thoughts and feelings.

Chapter Sixteen

BE DEDICATED

The Apostle Paul, who worked for more than thirty years bringing people to Christ as one of the greatest missionaries who ever lived, declared, "This one thing I do" (Philippians 3:13). He was following his Master's example in dedicating himself to the greatest cause on earth.

The Lord Jesus Christ wants you and me to do the same: dedicate ourselves and focus our lives on the things that matter most—the things of eternity. He taught that the eye is the light of the body and the window to the soul. If our eye is single,[1] if we are dedicated to our Savior's glorious cause, then our whole body will be full of light (D&C 88:67). He is our light, so our whole life can be filled with his influence, and no darkness will persist in us.

The Lord also taught that whatever you consider your "treasure," there is where your heart will be. There is where your thoughts and affections will be placed (Matthew 6:19–34; Luke

12:33–34; 3 Nephi 13:19–34; Helaman 8:25). He wants our hearts on him and on his work so that his work and glory become our work and glory.

The first and great commandments are to "have no other gods before me" (Exodus 20:3) and to "love the Lord thy God with all thine heart, and with all thy soul, and with all thy might" (Deuteronomy 6:5; 2 Nephi 25:29). From the beginning, top priority has always been given to love God above all other things and before all other persons. "And thou shalt love the Lord thy God with all thy heart, and with all thy soul, and with all thy mind, and with all thy strength" (Mark 12:30; Deuteronomy 6:4–5).

Christina Rossetti penned one of the loveliest verses I know:

> *What can I give Him,*
> *Poor as I am?*
> *If I were a shepherd*
> *I would bring a lamb.*
> *If I were a Wise Man*
> *I would do my part,*
> *Yet what can I give Him?*
> *Give my heart.*[2]

Christina Rossetti, and the rest of us, must give our hearts, our dedicated efforts, to build the kingdom of God. In fact, the Savior has said so in plain terms: "I, the Lord, *require* the hearts of the children of men" (D&C 64:22; emphasis added). Why does he demand our undivided attention on him and his work? Because of some egotistical need he has for total domination and glorification of himself? Not at all. His motives are pure and simple. He knows the Father's plan is the only way to eternal happiness and fulfillment, and there is no way to come unto the Father except through him, our Savior. It is to our everlasting advantage to set our hearts on him.

But you might think, "Well, I'm not actually dedicating all my efforts totally to building the kingdom because I have to go out and earn money." To that I would say that any honorable work you are doing to help feed and clothe and educate your family and raise up righteous children unto the Lord *is* the Lord's work. If you spend time regularly reading the scriptures and other good books and stories to each of your children, and you take a child to the ballpark, the golf course, the swimming pool, or the tennis court, and your effort is to stay close to that child and develop a lasting relationship, you are building the kingdom of God. All that you do by way of work or play could be beneficial to your family and others and thereby help build the kingdom.

Following a brief conversation with President James E. Faust one morning after breakfast in Jerusalem about my struggle to find a balance between academia and service (books versus people), President Faust said to me, "Your assignment is to change lives!"

That's it. That is the Lord's counsel to you too: "Your assignment is to change lives." Your priorities could be something like this: your spouse, your immediate family, your extended family, your Church family, your friends, and others.

Jesus was the Good Shepherd, and he left us his teachings about how we can follow his example and be shepherds too, caring for the sheep of his fold. There is a variety of ways: helping to keep some in the fold, bringing others into the fold, and bringing straying ones back into the fold. The religious leaders among the ancient Jews were regarded as, and were supposed to be, the shepherds of the people. They undoubtedly understood the rebuke in the adjective Jesus used: "I am the *good* shepherd." Then he said, "The good shepherd giveth his life for the sheep" (John 10:11; emphasis added), which is a true assessment of the dedicated shepherd out in the pastures and is a poignant foreshadowing of the Good Shepherd giving his life for his sheep.

The hireling sheepherder lacks personal interest and sincere concern for the sheep and at any sign of trouble may flee rather than risk his own life.

Stephen R. Covey wrote: "When the hired sheepherder fails or is criticized, he leaves his sheep: 'The hireling fleeth, because he is an hireling, and careth not for the sheep' (John 10:13). He leaves by giving excuses, by asking for other jobs, or by indifference and complacency. Sheepherder officers and teachers should not wonder why their attendance is low, why so many sheep are lost. If they're honest, they'll examine their own hearts and make changes."[3]

Jesus gave his all. Peter, James, John, Paul, and many others in former days gave their all. Joseph Smith and Brigham Young gave their all. A personal motto of Brigham Young and John Taylor was "The kingdom of God or nothing."[4] Joseph F. Smith said, "Personally, I have nothing but this cause to live for, for the rest of my life."[5] There is a host of outstanding exemplars who have dedicated their all for the purposes of God. We can learn how to do it too by studying their lives, especially the life of Jesus Christ, the highest and greatest Exemplar of all.

Isaac Watts was a prolific hymn-writer. He wrote the words of "Sweet Is the Work," "He Died! The Great Redeemer Died," "Joy to the World," and seven other hymns in the Latter-day Saint hymnbook. Another great hymn of his, not found in our hymnbook, is "When I Survey the Wondrous Cross." It contains one of the most powerful expressions of devotion he ever wrote:

> *When I survey the wondrous cross*
> *On which the Prince of glory died,*
> *My richest gain I count but loss,*
> *And pour contempt on all my pride.*
>
> *Forbid it, Lord, that I should boast,*
> *Save in the death of Christ, my God!*
> *All the vain things that charm me most,*
> *I sacrifice them to his blood.*
>
> *See, from his head, his hands, his feet,*
> *Sorrow and love flow mingled down!*
> *Did e'er such love and sorrow meet,*
> *Or thorns compose so rich a crown?*
>
> *Were the whole realm of nature mine,*
> *That were a present far too small;*
> *Love, so amazing, so divine,*
> *Demands my soul, my life, my all!*[6]

"Love, so amazing, so divine" does indeed demand your soul, your life, your all. The Savior wants your heart to be dedicated or consecrated to him. Another word for dedication is commitment. He wants us to be fully committed—not just "cultural Mormons" but real Latter-day Saints. It is not enough to be lukewarm in what the Prophet Joseph called "so great a cause" (D&C 128:22). As a matter of fact, the Lord indicates that he is disgusted with the behavior of anyone who is merely lukewarm (Revelation 3:16).

To better understand that strong image and others related to it, my friend and colleague Andrew Skinner and I traveled to western Turkey some years ago. We went to the region called Asia in the New Testament to investigate the meaning behind some interesting teachings Jesus gave through his beloved John to seven branches of the Church there. One of the Savior's figurative expressions particularly fascinated us: what he spoke to the Saints in Laodicea, which lies about a hundred miles east of the Aegean coastal city of Ephesus:

"I know thy works, that thou art neither cold nor hot: I would thou wert cold or hot. So then because thou art lukewarm, and neither cold nor hot, I will spue thee out of my mouth" (Revelation 3:15–16).

Brother Skinner and I learned that the Lycus Valley, where Laodicea is situated, features some excellent cold springs, good for a refreshing drink, and some extraordinary hot springs, good for therapeutic purposes. The cold water and the hot water were both good and useful ("I would thou wert cold or hot"). The Laodiceans, however, had brought in water through an aqueduct, at some considerable labor and expense, from another part of the valley. It turned out to be lukewarm water that became emetic (inducing vomiting).

We saw many pieces of that ancient stone aqueduct lying broken up in the surrounding fields. The pieces were all choked up, closed because of those mineral-laden, lukewarm waters.

The Lord Jesus and the Apostle John used that geographical phenomenon to illustrate how the cold waters and the hot waters, both helpful and prized, represented active members of the kingdom, producing much good. But the lukewarm waters were the uncommitted members who were and are unproductive and even destructive to the cause.

Again, the Savior wants you to be committed and dedicated to his labor of serving and saving souls. A more ancient example of a dedicated soul was the patriarch and dispensation head named Enoch, one of the remarkable personalities of all history. The English name Enoch in Hebrew is *Hanokh,* which literally means "dedicated." You may recognize the name in the Jewish holiday Hanukkah, which means "dedication"; John 10:22 reports that Jesus went up to Jerusalem at the feast of dedication during winter time, the end of December.

Enoch dedicated himself to raising his people to such a condition of righteousness that they didn't need to remain any longer in this telestial world and were translated to a terrestrial level. They have taken a five-thousand-year leave of absence from the earth, with God's promise that they will return to join others in the New Jerusalem during the great millennial era (JST, Genesis 14:34; Moses 7:18–21, 62–64; Ether 13:3).

Enoch's life story is recounted briefly in Moses 6 and 7. Modern revelation also preserves some uncommon information about this great prophet and seer; for instance, Doctrine and Covenants 107:49 tells us that Enoch "saw the Lord, and he walked with him, and was before his face continually."

Now, what could that last phrase—he was "before his face continually"—possibly mean? Apparently through prayer and the Lord's personal appearances, the prophet had continual contact with Deity. Enoch was, indeed, a dedicated man.

Jesus said to the Father, "I have finished the work which thou gavest me to do" (John 17:4). The Father has given you work to do also, and someday you can return and report to him that you finished that work.

The scriptures offer you a personal invitation to sup on a daily basis with all the noble and great ones and to become a *Hanokh,* a soul fully dedicated to the work of the Father—as Jesus was.

Chapter Seventeen
BE DISCIPLINED

We refer to Jesus Christ by many noble and meaningful titles, such as Creator, Redeemer, Lord, Savior, and Messiah. But one title stands out as impressively instructive for our permissive and loose generation: Jesus, *the Master*. Jesus showed himself master of the elements of nature and of all things outside himself, but he also demonstrated that he had totally mastered his own feelings, passions, and desires.

We often declare that one of our earth-life objectives is obtaining a body—but to do *what* with that body? To learn to control it.

We call Jesus *the Master* because he had perfect control of feelings of anger. Even when angered by the injustice and unrighteousness of religious leaders or merchandisers around sacred temple courts, he had total mastery of his rebuke. Centuries earlier Israel's first king, Saul, expressed uncontrolled feelings of anger, even to the point of murder.

Jesus had perfect control over feelings of jealousy and envy. Cain and Judas did not. Their lack of control led to grave, tragic sin.

Jesus had perfect control of sexual drives. One of ancient Israel's greatest spiritual and political leaders, King David, at his crucial moment of trial and test of character, gave way to uncontrolled illicit desire, even to the point of murder.

Jesus had perfect control of his body. He demonstrated complete self-mastery when he abstained from food and water for a long period of time in the desolate Judean wilderness. When wind and waves increased on the Sea of Galilee and grown men became frightened, Jesus could peacefully sleep amid the tempest.

Jesus was master of his mind, his tongue, his heart, his whole soul. And through a Book of Mormon prophet, he says to us, "Bridle all your passions, that ye may be filled with love" (Alma 38:12).

We should not be trying just to endure to the end of this life, hoping to make it successfully through moments of temptation in this world, thinking that maybe when we have passed into the next world the weak points of our character will automatically dissolve or disappear. Our object is not just to endure to the end; our object is to overcome evil feelings and tendencies *now*. The probation is here and now, and self-mastery is the crucial principle.

Jesus said, "I have overcome the world" (John 16:33). He had mastered himself, so he could beckon others to come unto him, to follow him. He is the Way, and while we are mastering self, we can reach out to others and help them find the Way.

No one achieves self-mastery overnight; it is a long process of struggling and overcoming. But we need to be sure we are on the right track and that we are moving forward—if we are just sitting there, we will be left behind. The Savior does not expect instant perfection, but he does expect continuous progress.

When we are disciplined, we are true disciples. Both *discipline* and *disciple* come from the Latin *discipulus. Discipline* means teaching, instruction, learning; *disciple* means the one who accepts the teaching, instruction, learning and then faithfully acts on it. The disciple devotedly follows the discipline.

In his great Sermon on the Mount (Matthew 5–7), Jesus explained several specific ways in which a disciple can properly live the gospel, the higher law. His examples illustrate a basic theme of the sermon: how to overcome the flesh—that is, how to learn to control the body. Jesus' examples teach us that we must learn to control our emotions (especially anger), our sexual desires (immoral thoughts and actions), our food intake (through fasting), and our tongue (verbal communication).

Included in the old law as one of the Ten Commandments was a commandment not to kill (Exodus 20:13).[1] That law, of course, still stands. But the higher law is to refrain from even getting angry (Matthew 5:21–22). The Savior charges us not to allow feelings of anger to get started that could lead to murder. Anger is a strong emotion. Note that anger is one letter short of *danger.* It is beyond irritation, annoyance, disgust, or other such feelings, which are also contrary to the spirit of the gospel; it is a deep, passionate wrath that could lead one to commit murder. Even a noble, righteous prophet like Nephi struggled with feelings of anger toward his enemies (his older brothers), and he knew that such intense feelings were wrong, sinful, and damaging to his spirituality (2 Nephi 4:17–31; see especially verses 17–19, 27–29). Nephi knew that anger was forbidden by the gospel of Jesus Christ, as is plainly expressed in Matthew 5:22. The Joseph Smith Translation of Ephesians 4:26 asks the relevant question, "Can ye be angry, and not sin?"

"We have seen that anger against another can only result after we commit sin (think unrighteously), but there is something in the nature of anger itself and its consequences that is also sinful. *Anger itself is a sin* when sin is defined as anything that retards the growth or progress of an individual."[2]

Elder ElRay L. Christiansen observed that "President Spencer W. Kimball, in his excellent book *The Miracle of Forgiveness,* tells us in effect that anger is 'a sin of thought' which, if not controlled, may be the forerunner of vicious and violent acts."[3]

Elder Theodore M. Burton warned: "Whenever you get red in the face, whenever you raise your voice, whenever you get 'hot under the collar,' or angry, rebellious, or negative in spirit, then know that the Spirit of God is leaving you and the spirit of Satan is beginning to take over. At times we may feel justified in arguing or fighting for truth by contentious words and actions. Do not be deceived."[4]

Similarly, Sister Ogden noted while we were in Guatemala: "Anger, irritation, annoyance—all from below. My, how the devil loves to separate people: spouses from each other, children from parents, ward members from each other, brothers and sisters, etc.

[BYU colleague] Catherine Thomas said that the reason we have abrasive people in our lives is so we can learn to develop divine love. This life is a laboratory for practicing divine love. And until we get the hang of it, we will have one irritating person after another come into our lives to give us plenty of practice."[5]

Also included in the old law was a commandment not to commit adultery (Exodus 20:14). That law, too, still stands. But the higher law is for individuals never even to lust after another (Matthew 5:27–28). If they do, they have already committed adultery in their hearts. If you do not allow lustful feelings to get started that could lead to adultery, you will never have to worry about that great sin. Once again, as Alma encouraged his son, "Bridle all your passions, that ye may be filled with love" (Alma 38:12). If we are full of genuine love, there is no room for lust. If we control the first tempting urges to accommodate physical desires, then we will not follow through and succumb to the serious sexual sin. The Savior reiterated the same commandment in our day, with added warnings of consequences for violating it:

"Verily I say unto you, as I have said before, he that looketh on a woman to lust after her, or if any shall commit adultery in their hearts, they shall not have the Spirit, but shall deny the faith and shall fear" (D&C 63:16).

You are obligated by the gospel of Christ to eventually overcome all temptations, big and small. The teachings of Jesus on the mount are big, but smaller issues are also important, as illustrated by Elder M. Russell Ballard:

"'Wo unto him that has the law given, . . . that wasteth the days of his probation' (2 Nephi 9:27). . . .

"'Thou shalt not idle away thy time . . . ' (D&C 60:13). Why would I speak of that with you? Because one of the ways Satan lessens your effectiveness and weakens your spiritual strength is by encouraging you to spend large blocks of your time doing things that matter very little. I speak of such things as sitting for hours on end watching television or videos, playing video games night in and night out, surfing the Internet, or devoting huge blocks of time to sports, games, or other recreational activities.

"Don't misunderstand me. These activities are not wrong in and of themselves (unless, of course, you are watching salacious programs or seeking out pornographic images on the Internet). Games, sports, recreational activities, and even television can be relaxing and rejuvenating, especially in times when you are under stress or heavily scheduled. You need activities that help you to unwind and rest your minds. It is healthy to go onto the soccer field or the basketball court and participate in vigorous physical activity.

"But I speak of letting things get out of balance. It is not watching television, but watching television hour after hour, night after night. Does not that qualify as idling away your time? What will you say to the Lord when He asks what you have done with the precious gift of life and time? Surely you will not feel comfortable telling Him that you were able to pass the 100,000-point level in a challenging video game.

"One devastating effect of idling away our time is that it deflects us from focusing on the things that matter most. Too many people are willing to sit back and let life just happen to them.

It takes time to develop the attributes that will help you to be a well-balanced person."[6]

The purpose of all these laws, big and little, is to help you become like Jesus and like your Father in Heaven. You want to show them that you are a person of integrity, that you can be trusted with higher and higher things.

My son Daniel was in Europe several years ago on assignment from the United States government to conduct interviews of U.S. military personnel and civilians, along with a few civilians from other countries, for top-secret clearance. He described the interview questions to me in some detail, and I concluded that they were far more extensive than a Latter-day Saint's temple recommend interview. Before he even sat down with those he interviewed, Daniel had in his possession their police records, national agency records, financial records, credit reports, and so on.

Daniel probed where they had been, whom they had been with, and why. He had to inquire if they had ever used drugs or alcohol (how much and how often), if they had ever been convicted of any crime, or if they had ever been divorced, been involved in any sexual misconduct, had any extramarital affairs, or been guilty of any abuse. Daniel had to have details of any and all debt. The searching questions were designed to establish the person's loyalty and honesty. The basic idea of the interviewing process was to answer the question "Can this person be trusted?"

What an interesting phenomenon from a gospel perspective. Isn't that exactly what will happen to you as you pass into the eternal worlds to be judged in regard to your earth life? Aren't you here to be cleared for capacity and worthiness to receive all the top secrets of godliness and prove that you can be trusted to perform work similar to that done by our Heavenly Father?

Elder Melvin J. Ballard said, "A man may receive the priesthood and all its privileges and blessings, but until he learns to overcome the flesh, his temper, his tongue, his disposition to indulge in the things God has forbidden, he cannot come into the celestial kingdom of God."[7] After all, God's eternal plan is not the plan of pleasure; it is the plan of happiness. True happiness requires control and self-mastery.

The discipline of earth life is to prepare for the work and glory of eternity, and eternity is a long time to think about a job *not* well done. So learn here and now to be a true disciple, to be disciplined—like Jesus.

Chapter Eighteen

BE CHRISTLIKE

Centuries after giving the Israelites of the Mosaic era a law of carnal commandments (D&C 84:27)—"a very strict law . . . a law of performances and of ordinances" (Mosiah 13:29–30)—Jesus Christ came personally to give his people a higher law, as epitomized in his great Sermon on the Mount (Matthew 5–7). He raised the bar on what he expected of his true disciples, his covenant people.

Remember the Lord's declaration that "I am the light of the world" (John 8:12). He also wants us to be the light of the world, which is a high standard to live by. Many good Christian people have lived, and are now living, with the hope of emulating the Savior's example and becoming as he is. Mother Teresa raised the bar on Christian behavior when she put the following poem on the walls of the orphanage she established in Calcutta:

People are illogical, unreasonable, and self-centered.
Love them anyway.

If you do good, people will accuse you of selfish
    ulterior motives.
Do good anyway.
. . . .

The good you do today will be forgotten tomorrow.
Do good anyway.

Honesty and frankness make you vulnerable.
Be honest and frank anyway.
. . . .

Give the world the best you have and you'll get
    kicked in the teeth.
Give the world the best you have anyway.[1]

My two favorite expressions in Latin are *lux lucet in tenebras* and *post tenebras lux.* The first, *lux lucet in tenebras,* was translated into King James English as "the light shineth in darkness" (John 1:5). Jesus taught, "Let your light so shine before men, that they may see your good works, and glorify your Father which is in heaven" (Matthew 5:16).

The Savior gave to his disciples the charge to be the light for all people. We are many lights now, a large city, and we cannot be hid. We are conspicuous lights in this world of darkness. As a candle or lamp is put on a candlestick or lamp stand (a *menorah* in Hebrew), so we must set our light to shine throughout our communities and nations: "Let your light so shine before men." Jesus Christ is our light, for he said, "I am the light which ye shall hold up" (3 Nephi 18:24). In other words, our objective is to let him, our Light, shine through us to the glory of the Father, not for our own glory. As Jesus said, we are the light of the world but only in the sense that we allow him to shine through us.

He told his ancient followers, "The eyes of the blind shall see out of obscurity and out of darkness" (Isaiah 29:18), but if we do not ask, knock, and inquire, we are not brought into the light but must perish in the dark (2 Nephi 32:4). Peter advised the disciples of Jesus, "We have also a more sure word of prophecy; whereunto ye do well that ye take heed, as unto a light that shineth in a dark place" (2 Peter 1:19).

There is a lot of darkness in our world now, but the Savior's light still shines bright. Said Jesus in our day, "If your eye be single to my glory, your whole bodies shall be filled with light, and there shall be no darkness in you; and that body which is filled with light comprehendeth all things" (D&C 88:67).

Satan doesn't turn the lights off all at once; he uses a dimmer switch. If you are not careful to recognize what the devil is doing, your light can gradually go out. As you faithfully follow the Savior, however, you continually fill your soul with light, "and he that receiveth light, and continueth in God, receiveth more light; and that light groweth brighter and brighter until the perfect day" (D&C 50:24).

We are living examples of my other favorite Latin phrase, *post tenebras lux,* which was the motto of the Protestants during the Reformation and is inscribed on the Reformer's Wall in Geneva, Switzerland. The phrase means "after the darkness, light." Just as young Joseph Smith experienced in the grove of trees, first came "thick darkness" and then came brilliant light (Joseph

Smith–History 1:15). In our day, just as in Isaiah's day and in Jesus' day, "people that walked in darkness have seen a great light" (Isaiah 9:2). Alma adds, "They were in the midst of darkness; nevertheless, their souls were illuminated by the light" (Alma 5:7).

Living in the light brings happiness, peace, and strength to endure the dark moments of this temporary mortality. As Peter exclaimed, "[You] should shew forth the praises of him who hath called you out of darkness into his marvellous light" (1 Peter 2:9).

We sing, "I'm trying to be like Jesus."[2] Why? Because he is our example in all things. "What manner of men ought ye *to be?* . . . Even as *I am*" (3 Nephi 27:27; emphasis added).

Jesus has laid out a clear pattern of how to live, here and forever. He is the personification of all noble character traits. He is—so he wants us to be—happy, holy, spiritually minded, humble, knowledgeable, serviceable, prayerful, peaceful, fruitful, obedient, loving, forgiving, long-suffering, persevering, united with him and his Father, dedicated, disciplined, and Christlike.

He came to show us how to live. His teachings are the perfect lessons; his life is the perfect lesson. Leona B. Gates put the purpose and message of his life in the following beautiful verses under the title "In His Steps":

> *The road is rough, I said,*
> *Dear Lord, there are stones that hurt me so.*
> *And he said, Dear child, I understand,*
> *I walked it long ago.*
>
> *But there is a cool green path, I said,*
> *Let me walk there for a time.*

No child, He gently answered me,
The green road does not climb.

My burden, I said, is far too great;
How can I bear it so?
My child, said he, I remember weight.
I carried my cross, you know.

But, I said, I wish there were friends with me
Who would make my way their own.
Ah, yes, he said, Gethsemane
Was hard to face alone.

And so I climbed the stony path,
Content at last to know
That where my Master had not gone
I would not need to go.

And strangely then I found new friends;
The burden grew less sore
As I remembered—long ago
He [walked this] way before.[3]

When the seeming calamities and hard trials of our lives draw
out noisy responses of complaint and objection from our hearts
and lips, the Lord reminds us to "be still and know that I am
God." And he says to us, "*I am* your Savior; *I am* your Redeemer;
I am your Comforter. So be still and know. *I am,* so *you be.*"

As we learn and live all the attributes of our Savior we briefly
discussed, we will indeed be happy—like Jesus.

Notes

Introduction

1. Smith, *History of the Church,* 4:588.

2. Jefferson, *Character of Jesus,* 9–10, 21–22.

Chapter One: Be Happy

1. Kimball, *Journal of Discourses,* 4:222.

2. Smith, *History of the Church,* 1:280.

3. Holland, "Come unto Me," 190.

4. Marshall, quoted in Uldrich, *Soldier, Statesman, Peacemaker,* 216.

5. Smith, *History of the Church,* 2:381.

6. Hinckley, quoted in Holland, "President Gordon B. Hinckley," 12.

Chapter Two: Be Holy

1. Ogden, Mission Journal, June 18, 2006.

2. *Holiness* is inscribed on all of the Lord's temples. Although the usual translation in English is "holy house" (1 Chronicles 29:3; D&C 96:2; 110:8; 124:39), the Hebrew expression is actually "house of holiness" (*beit hakodesh*). It is the same with Heavenly Father's name or title. He is not just a "holy man" but rather a "Man of

Holiness" (Moses 6:57; 7:35). Also, it should not be just a "holy city" (Nehemiah 11:1, 18) but rather a "City of Holiness" (Moses 7:19; *ir hakodesh* in Hebrew). Nor should it be merely a "holy land" (Zechariah 2:12) but rather a "land of holiness" (*admat hakodesh* in Hebrew). Altogether we might describe this concept in the following way: our eminent objective for a millennial era foresees us being a covenant people of holiness worshiping a Man of Holiness in a house of holiness, in a city of holiness, in a land of holiness.

Chapter Three: Be Spiritually Minded

1. Packer, *Mine Errand from the Lord,* 126–27.
2. Packer, "The One Pure Defense," 7.
3. Packer, *Holy Temple,* 265.

Chapter Four: Be Humble

1. See LDS Bible Dictionary, "John the Baptist," 714.
2. Eyring, *To Draw Closer to God,* 110.
3. Bednar, address to religious educators, as quoted in Lund, *Hearing the Voice of the Lord,* 226.
4. Brown, "Currant Bush," 14–15.

Chapter Five: Be Knowledgeable

1. For many years I have enjoyed and shared with my students the great story from Dr. Agassiz included in this chapter. Recently I learned even more reasons why I like the man and his teachings. Author David McCullough, in an essay titled "The American Adventure of Louis Agassiz," writes:

   "It was another emphatic declaration by the master naturalist that there need be no conflict between the revelation of science and Genesis. 'Agassiz belongs to that class of naturalists who see God in everything,' wrote a reviewer. . . . Agassiz had described the whole of creation as an expression of 'divine thought.' . . .

"'Don't you perceive that if [Charles Darwin's] theory were true it would leave one without a God?' . . . Agassiz, who seldom went to church, denounced [Darwin's] book and its theory as atheism. . . .

"For Agassiz . . . to study nature was to study the works of God. He had little use for formal religion because, as he once wrote . . . , he had seen too much in his life of overbearing clerics and religious bigotry. But there could be no evolutionary process as depicted by Darwin for the simple reason that all species were special, distinct, fixed creations. Species—caterpillars, caribou, Lake Superior pike, or Darwin's finches—were the immutable aspects of the divine plan, which from the start had a specific final purpose, mankind. 'It can be shown that in the great plan of creation . . . the very commencement exhibits a certain tendency toward the end. . . . The constantly increasing similarity to man of the creatures successively called into existence makes the final purpose obvious.'

"Progress there had been, the long record of life on Earth was indeed an upward path. The changes, however, had been achieved, he insisted, in great creative stages . . . with man the crowning creation.

"Darwin's theory, Agassiz instructed the members of the Boston Society of Natural History, was 'ingenious but fanciful.' 'The resources of the Deity,' he wrote, 'cannot be so meager that in order to create a human being endowed with reason, He must change a monkey into a man.'

"[One of Agassiz' mottos was:] 'God's word and God's works mutually illustrating each other.'

"Agassiz of Harvard decried the theories of Charles Darwin, that he, of all learned men, marched foremost in the assault on the new godless vision of life" (*Brave Companions,* 29, 31, 32–33).

2. Hanks, "Good Teachers Matter," 61–62.

3. See Ogden and Ogden, *President and the Preacher II,* 105–6.

Chapter Six: Be Serviceable

1. Ogden and Skinner, *Verse by Verse,* 530.
2. Ehat and Cook, *Words of Joseph Smith,* 18n7.

Chapter Seven: Be Prayerful

1. Webster, *American Dictionary,* "importune."
2. Ehat and Cook, *Words of Joseph Smith,* 15.
3. Brown, quoted in Hartshorn, *Outstanding Stories by General Authorities,* 1:5–8.

Chapter Eight: Be Peaceful

1. Emerson, "Self-Reliance," in *Essays of Ralph Waldo Emerson,* 31.
2. Wiesel, quoted in Harvey, "Jesus in Medieval and Modern Jewish Thought."

Chapter Nine: Be Fruitful

1. Holland, "Abide in Me," 32.

Chapter Eleven: Be Loving

1. See Ogden, *8 Mighty Changes,* 138.
2. Ogden, Mission Journal, March 3, 2006.

Chapter Twelve: Be Forgiving

1. Ogden, Mission Journal, April 12, 2006.
2. Smith, *History of the Church,* 5:498.
3. Smith, *Gospel Doctrine,* 255–56.
4. Rowen, *21 Healing Secrets.*
5. Smith, *History of the Church,* 5:23–24.

Chapter Thirteen: Be Long-Suffering

1. Smith, *History of the Church,* 3:294.
2. Young, *Discourses of Brigham Young,* 345.
3. Young, *Discourses of Brigham Young,* 346.
4. Taylor, in *Journal of Discourses,* 24:197.

5. Cannon, *Gospel Truth*, 81.

6. Whitney, quoted in Kimball, *Faith Precedes the Miracle*, 98.

7. Kimball, *Faith Precedes the Miracle*, 98.

8. Packer, "Choice," 21; emphasis added.

9. Maxwell, "Lest Ye Be Wearied," 88.

10. Price, in *All Things Testify of Him*, 90; emphasis added; see also David O. McKay, "Pioneer Women," *Relief Society Magazine*, January 1948, 8; Faust, "Refiner's Fire," 53.

11. Faust, "Refiner's Fire," 53.

12. Romney, in Conference Report, October 1969, 60.

Chapter Fourteen: Be Persevering

1. Smith, *History of the Church*, 1:252–53.

2. Ogden and Skinner, *Verse by Verse*, 600–2.

Chapter Fifteen: Be United

1. Ogden, Mission Journal, January 17, 1999.

2. Ogden, Mission Journal, September 26, 2006.

3. Talmage, quoted in Ehat and Cook, *Words of Joseph Smith*, 137n4; order of sentences altered.

4. Talmage, quoted in Ehat and Cook, *Words of Joseph Smith*, 137n4.

5. Ogden, Mission Journal, October 3, 2006.

Chapter Sixteen: Be Dedicated

1. Joseph Smith added "to the glory of God" to this phrase (JST, Matthew 6:22; see also D&C 4:5).

2. Rossetti, quoted in Lyon, et al., *Best-Loved Poems*, 166–67.

3. Covey, quoted in Millet, *Redeemer*, 110.

4. Young, *Discourses of Brigham Young*, 444; Taylor, *John Taylor*, 221.

5. Smith, in Conference Report, April 1912, 2.

6. Isaac Watts wrote "When I Survey the Wondrous Cross" in 1707.

CHAPTER SEVENTEEN: BE DISCIPLINED

1. The Hebrew verb *ratzakh* means "to murder, to slay with premeditation."
2. Kelly, "Case against Anger," 10.
3. Christiansen, "Be Slow to Anger," 37.
4. Burton, "Blessed Are the Peacemakers," 56.
5. See Ogden and Ogden, *President and the Preacher II,* 177.
6. Ballard, "Be Strong in the Lord," 13–14.
7. Ballard, quoted in Kimball, *Miracle of Forgiveness,* 168.

CHAPTER EIGHTEEN: BE CHRISTLIKE

1. Keith, "The Paradoxical Commandments."
2. "I'm Trying to Be like Jesus," *Children's Songbook,* 78.
3. Gates, quoted in Lyon, et al., *Best-Loved Poems,* 179.

Sources

Ballard, M. Russell. "Be Strong in the Lord." *Ensign,* July 2004, 8–15.

Benson, Ezra Taft. "Listen to a Prophet's Voice." *Ensign*, January 1973, 57–59.

Brown, Hugh B. "The Currant Bush." *New Era,* January 1973, 14–15.

Burton, Theodore M. "'Blessed Are the Peacemakers.'" *Ensign,* November 1974, 54–56.

Cannon, George Q. *Gospel Truth: Discourses and Writings of George Q. Cannon.* Compiled by Jerreld L. Newquist. Classics in Mormon Literature series. Salt Lake City: Deseret Book, 1974.

Children's Songbook. Salt Lake City: The Church of Jesus Christ of Latter-day Saints, 1989.

Christiansen, ElRay L. "Be Slow to Anger." *Ensign,* June 1971, 37–38.

Conference Reports of The Church of Jesus Christ of Latter-day Saints. Salt Lake City: The Church of Jesus Christ of Latter-day Saints, 1898–present.

Ehat, Andrew F., and Lyndon W. Cook, eds. *The Words of Joseph Smith.* Orem, Utah: Grandin Book, 1991.

Emerson, Ralph Waldo. *Essays of Ralph Waldo Emerson.* Edited by Alfred R. Ferguson and Jean Ferguson Carr, with an introduction by Alfred Kazin. Cambridge, Mass.: Belknap Press of Harvard Press, 1987.

Eyring, Henry B. *To Draw Closer to God.* Salt Lake City: Deseret Book, 1997.

Faust, James E. "The Refiner's Fire." *Ensign,* May 1979, 53–59.

Hanks, Marion D. "Good Teachers Matter." *Ensign,* July 1971, 60–64.

Hartshorn, Leon R., comp. *Outstanding Stories by General Authorities.* 3 vols. Salt Lake City: Deseret Book, 1970–74.

Harvey, Zeev. "Jesus in Medieval and Modern Jewish Thought." Israeli government-sponsored seminar on Christ, at Sedom, Israel, March 23–25, 1990; personal notes by D. Kelly Ogden.

Holland, Jeffrey R. "Abide in Me." *Ensign,* May 2004, 30–32.

———. "Come unto Me." *Speeches, 1996–97.* Provo, Utah: Brigham Young University, 1997.

———. "President Gordon B. Hinckley: Stalwart and Brave He Stands." *Ensign,* June 1995, 2–13.

Jefferson, Charles Edward. *The Character of Jesus.* New York: Thomas Y. Crowell, 1908.

Journal of Discourses. 26 vols. Liverpool: Latter-day Saints' Book Depot, 1854–86.

Keith, Kent M. "The Paradoxical Commandments," at http://www.paradoxicalcommandments.com; see also http://www.paradoxicalchristians.com; accessed 7 February 2011. © 1968 Kent M. Keith, renewed 2001. Used by permission.

Kelly, Burton C. "The Case against Anger." *Ensign,* February 1980, 9–12.

Kimball, Spencer W. *Faith Precedes the Miracle.* Salt Lake City: Deseret Book, 1972.

———. *The Miracle of Forgiveness.* Salt Lake City: Deseret Book, 1969.

Lund, Gerald N. *Hearing the Voice of the Lord.* Salt Lake City: Deseret Book, 2007.

Lyon, Jack, et al., eds. *Best-Loved Poems of the LDS People.* Salt Lake City: Deseret Book, 1996.

Maxwell, Neal A. "'Lest Ye Be Wearied and Faint in Your Minds.'" *Ensign,* May 1991, 88–91.

McCullough, David. *Brave Companions—Portraits in History.* New York: Simon and Schuster, 1992.

McKay, David O. "Pioneer Women." *Relief Society Magazine,* January 1948, 4–9.

Millet, Robert L. *The Redeemer: Reflections on the Life and Teachings of Jesus the Christ.* Salt Lake City: Deseret Book, 2000.

Ogden, D. Kelly. *8 Mighty Changes God Wants for You Before You Get to Heaven.* Salt Lake City: Deseret Book, 2004.

Ogden, D. Kelly, and Andrew C. Skinner. *Verse by Verse: The Four Gospels.* Salt Lake City: Deseret Book, 2006.

Ogden, D. Kelly, and Marcia H. Ogden. *The President and the Preacher II: Memoirs of a Missionary Training Center President and Companion.* Published by the authors, 2008.

Packer, Boyd K. "The Choice." *Ensign,* November 1980, 20–22.

———. *The Holy Temple.* Salt Lake City: Bookcraft, 1980.

———. *Mine Errand from the Lord.* Salt Lake City: Deseret Book, 2008.

———. "The One Pure Defense." *Religious Educator* 5, no. 2 (2004): 1–11.

Price, Clark Kelley. In *All Things Testify of Him—Inspirational Paintings by Latter-day Saint Artists.* Salt Lake City: Bookcraft, 1998.

Rowen, Robert Jay. *21 Healing Secrets Your Alternative Doctor Doesn't Know About.* Atlanta, Ga.: Second Opinion, 2007.

Smith, Joseph. *History of The Church of Jesus Christ of Latter-day Saints.* Edited by B. H. Roberts. 2d ed. rev. 7 vols. Salt Lake City: The Church of Jesus Christ of Latter-day Saints, 1932–51.

Smith, Joseph F. *Gospel Doctrine: Selections from the Sermons and Writings of Joseph F. Smith*. Salt Lake City: Deseret Book, 1939.

Talmage, James E. "The Eternity of Sex." *Young Woman's Journal* 25 (October 1914): 602–3, as quoted in Ehat and Cook, *Words of Joseph Smith*.

Taylor, John. *John Taylor*. Teachings of Presidents of the Church series. Salt Lake City: The Church of Jesus Christ of Latter-day Saints, 2001.

Uldrich, Jack. *Soldier, Statesman, Peacemaker—Leadership Lessons from George C. Marshall*. New York: Amacom, 2005.

Webster, Noah. *An American Dictionary of the English Language*. 1828. Reprint. San Francisco: Foundation for American Christian Education, 1980.

Young, Brigham, *Discourses of Brigham Young*. Selected by John A. Widtsoe. Salt Lake City: Deseret Book, 1971.

Index